BY-PASS ROAD

ACRUM

NNEY

II RECREATION GROUND

GASWORKS

7

ER ITCHEN

8

9

10

RAILWAY

NUNS WALK

II

ABBOTS
BARTON

WINCHESTER

Scale 6"-1 mile

Itchen
Memories

ITCHEN MEMORIES

G.E.M. SKUES

With Illustrations by
ALEX JARDINE

ROBERT HALE · LONDON

ISBN 978 0 7090 6372 8

Robert Hale Limited
Clerkenwell House
Clerkenwell Green
London EC1R 0HT

www.halebooks.com

A catalogue record for this book is available from the British Library

Printed and bound in Great Britain by TJ International Ltd

Publisher's Note

Despite the best efforts of this company and other publishers it has proved impossible to trace any beneficiaries of the Estate of G.E.M. Skues. Rather than allow the classic *Itchen Memories* to disappear, this company decided to reissue the book and to make provision for the payment of standard royalties in the hope that, at some date, any beneficiaries will make themselves known to us.

There is some debate about whether it should be Abbotts or Abbots Barton. 'Abbotts' has been adopted in this book to reflect the spelling which is currently used by the Abbotts Barton Fishery.

Introduction

————◀o▶————

ITCHEN MEMORIES is not a general collection of fishing
memoirs concerning past days spent along various Itchen
beats. It concerns just one, specific, length of this lovely chalk
stream. The watery maze of carriers, ditches and drains which
criss-cross Winchester's northern water-meadows, for centuries
known as Abbotts Barton, is the sole setting for the collection of
stories which follow. It is a final and cherished selection of memories and meanderings of fifty-seven long seasons spent among
AB's lush meadows rich with marsh flowers where, on still
summer evenings, the air hangs heavy with the scent of meadow-
sweet and water-mint bruised by the stalking angler's boot. It was
in these surroundings that, from 1883 to 1938, George Edward
Mackenzie Skues developed his frequently challenged method of
nymph fishing, spending as much time there as his busy London
law practice would allow. Abbotts Barton became his spiritual
home, his first and last love.

G.E.M. Skues was to his friends a kind and generous host who,
in terms of appearance, was comical and ungainly. Yet as an angler
he possessed a powerfully analytical mind which placed him in a
league occupied by few other angler/writers, past or present. He
had the ability to look beyond the simple pleasures or frustrations
of days spent in tranquil meadows, to analyse the subtle reasons

for success or failure and, moreover, to find delightful words to illustrate his conclusions.

Itchen Memories was possibly the outcome of some lengthy soul-searching towards the end of a long life when he realised time was short. I can only imagine that with a multitude of memories fluttering through his mind like a cloud of evening sedge flies, his shaky hands conjured the ghosts and phantoms of many long happy summers. These handwritten notes were deposited with his younger brother Charles accompanied by the strict instruction that they were to be published only after his death. Although corrections have been made, wherever possible, to this latest edition, without G.E.M.S. to check the translation of his scrawled manuscript all those years ago, some errors may remain within the text of the original work.

It was coincidental that Charles Skues had an angler/artist friend who occupied an office within the same London building. It was thus that the late Alex Jardine, father of the talented modern painter of angling scenes, Charles Jardine, was asked to illustrate the book. It was with great pleasure that I learned of the publisher's intention to retain the original sketches in this new edition. I came to know Alex quite well and we spent some happy hours discussing our mutual love for the Itchen over many a pink gin. A few years after his father's death, Charles, very generously, gave me the original drawing of the trout beneath the pussy-willows which appears in this book. As you may well imagine, this is now one of my greatest treasures.

The birthplace of modern nymph fishing is not the only accolade of which Abbotts Barton boasts. Between 1879 and 1882 that other great angler/writer Francis Francis leased the water in company with George Selwyn Marryat. During these years Marryat, H.S. Hall and Dr Sanctuary did much of their work putting the finishing touches to the dressing and fishing of what we now know as the modern dry fly. Marryat first met F.M. Halford in John Hammond's shop in the Square in Winchester in April 1879. It was to be some seven years later that *Floating Flies and How to Dress Them* hit the angling world like a whirlwind. However, it seems beyond doubt that those first, truly dry flies had been originated years earlier by Marryat & Co. along Itchen's marshy margins at Abbotts Barton.

Skues occasionally described the fishery as "not one of the crack dry fly stretches of the Test or Kennet, but it is intimate and homely". It certainly was, and still is, a great mixture of slow deep lengths, medium paced, canal-like stretches contrasted here and there by the chuckling raceways of the west to east streams. Once described by William Senior as "one of the most difficult waters within my experience", Abbotts Barton trout can certainly be tricky. At times, particularly from midsummer, the fish can display an uncanny ability to detect the angler's presence from an unbelievably distant approach, however cautiously stalked. Many times have I suffered the ignominy of crawling on all fours, to gain the cover of some clump of marginal sedge at such distance from the dimpling trout as to seem totally secure, only to find that the simple act of raising the rod to the horizontal in order to release the fly from its keeper-ring, was sufficient to ensure that the fish would rise no more.

From the time of the Francis and Marryat lease and for many of the years that G.E.M.S. fished, firstly as the guest of Mr I.B. Cox, and then later as a member of the little syndicate which he and H.T. Sheringham had formed, the upstream boundary was defined as the Kings Worthy sawmill on the Barton carrier to the west of the meadows. The upper boundary of the main river Itchen was marked by the confluence of a side-carrier with the mainstream, known as the "Half-water", about two or three hundred yards above the old railway bridge. The "Half-water" was known by G.E.M.S. as the *Trait d'Union* and is the length to which he refers in the chapter entitled "Three Grayling". The fishery's downstream boundaries were provided by Winchester's North Walls for the carriers and Durngate Mill sluices on the mainstream. To the west, above the city limits, parkland rolled east from Abbotts Barton House down to the old Tudor farmhouse and water-meadows. The eastern boundary was formed by the Great Western railway line just beyond which the Winchester gasworks was sited. Skues often referred to his fishery as being "as good a two and a half miles as anywhere". In truth he measured the length of only the main river. The extent of his carrier fishing would have more than trebled the fishable water to which he enjoyed access.

In 1932 he was separated from his upper lengths by the construction of the Winchester bypass which was, reputedly, the first such city bypass road in this country but was to remain unfinished until sometime after the second world war. The new upper boundary now formed by this road is still the fishery's upper limit. In more recent years alteration to the London road and A34 to and from the Midlands necessitated changes to the course of the Barton carrier and with it went the old sawmill also burying William Mullins's cottage under tons of concrete and asphalt. Skues left the little syndicate at the end of the 1938 season to take up fishing near Salisbury on the river Nadder. It was a move he felt bound to make due, in part, to changes in attitudes within the syndicate. He suffered objections to his nymph fishing and further restrictions on his guests, whom he loved to have. So after fifty-six years he dismantled his nine-foot, five-ounce Leonard, known affectionately as "World's Best Rod", and shambled off into the autumn dusk.

G.E.M.S. fished the river Nadder and, occasionally, the Wylye, for about seven years during which time he frequently complained of the damage done to these streams by the "Catchment Boards" who completely changed the nature of so many rivers by over-dredging and re-grading. Had he have known that the same was to happen to his favourite lengths of the main Itchen at AB (sometime in the early sixties) he would not have gone easy to his grave in 1949. The work was probably undertaken in order to alleviate flooding but the result was to increase the river's overall depth, reduce its width and decrease its potential to hold and nurture trout. It would also seem that no alteration of the stream's gradient took place with the further result that, in places, mud settled faster than ever.

The syndicate continued with William Mullins, who had succeeded John Locke and Humphry Priddis as its keeper, until about 1953 when it was disbanded and a twenty-one-year lease taken by the Piscatorial Society. This arrangement survived for almost fifteen years until, in 1970, the lower portion of the meadows was compulsorily purchased for "civic improvement" by the city council. A number of Skues's well-loved spots, locations such as the Red Hole, which is a deep pool formed by water pouring from the Park Stream through a set of red-brick culverts and almost adjacent to the old city bathing place, were now beyond his boundary. The Red Hole is at the head of a carrier known as Swift Lake. Also isolated from the existing beats is McCaskie's Corner where the main Itchen swerves even further eastward towards the now demolished little church of Winnal St Magdalene. Mac's corner and the deep millhead behind the cottages above Durngate mill, where the huge, impossible, old adversaries of G.E.M.S. would teasingly rise, are now part of a publicly accessible nature walk for modern Wintonians, with the fishing unmanaged and disallowed.

At some time between 1963 and 1970 the Barrow-Simmonds family sold off their lovely Abbotts Barton house and the adjoining land. The house became offices and the parkland was developed for housing. On the eastern side of the valley the old railway line was torn up and the gasworks replaced with a small modern industrial estate. I daresay Skues would have greatly preferred the smelly gasworks. Fortunately, a protective screen of trees was planted along the line of the factories and now, when in full leaf, these do much to prevent any great offence to the angler's view.

A hotchpotch of short-term leases followed with little or no keepering until the winter of 1973. Then, in some crazed moment of impractical zeal, my brother Ron and I, mellowed by numerous glasses of home-made elderberry wine consumed in the kitchen of the owner Mrs Whitfield, agreed to take a three-year lease of what had become derelict fishing. Our first season commenced in April 1974 and the task list became longer with every visit. Funds were very limited and the prospect of letting rods with the fishery in such poor condition was highly doubtful. However, a handful of trusting souls agreed to part with a hundred pounds or so and our first season got under way.

The years of neglect had taken their toll on the overall health and viability of the water. Huge deposits of mud had suffocated most of the desirable weedbeds. Most of the spawning gravels were compacted which had reduced the water's ability to support natural trout regeneration. As a result, native trout stocks were very poor. In addition most of the old sluices had fallen into disrepair, two of which, crucially, directed water from the mainstream and the Barton carrier into the middle stream called "Five-hatches". The result was that this stretch was reduced to a mere trickle between dense beds of reeds. Needless to say precious few trout were caught that first season despite our ill-afforded implant of a couple of hundred stock fish. Conditions were such that trout would either leave the water or were summarily eaten by the hordes of pike which infested the place.

Within five years a small circle of keen friends formed who also shared our dream and much more effort could therefore be utilised. Gradually, as the fishing improved, more rods were attracted and realistic charges could be levied. This increased our income and allowed us to afford machinery to dredge out Five-hatches and rebuild those vital sluices, as well as other major works. The day we opened the new sluice-gates for the first time was a great milestone in the fortunes of AB. At last Five-hatches flowed again and in the following season trout were once again to be caught along its length.

From the day I first walked the hallowed streams of Abbotts Barton it had always seemed a great tragedy that there was no mark to record its illustrious past and especially that no words recorded the fifty-six years occupancy of the great man. It was therefore a momentous occasion when, in August 1980, we asked G.E.M.S.'s great-nephew, Keith Skues, to inaugurate a memorial stone seat to his great uncle's memory. The seat had been provided by funds donated by the fishing public through an international appeal. The "Skues seat" and its sheltering willow now stand opposite the spot on the main river where, in 1949, Mullins the keeper scattered the ashes of one of the most significant figures in the history of fishing for trout with a fly.

Also in 1980 the eastern meadows with the fishing on the main-stream and Five-hatches came under the hammer. The owner had found it convenient to dispose of this section of the property and it was sold to a conservation organisation, the Hampshire and Isle of Wight Naturalists' Trust (now the Hampshire Wildlife Trust). During the tender period our rods formed a small bidding group, and made an unsuccessful offer to purchase the fishing rights only. Fortunately we were able to negotiate a long-term lease with the new owners. These events caused us to re-form as a club which continued until 1993 when I withdrew due to my increasing frustration with the encumbrances of management by committee. My close friend Stewart Newell, a rod and helpmate since 1975, supported me and fresh leases were successfully obtained in our joint names. The Abbotts Barton fishery was, yet again, launched into a new era.

Somehow the streams, the meadows and the fishery, as a whole, have responded to the love and care they have received. Thanks to the generous efforts of so many friends we have been able to wrest this famous place from the ravages of neglect and insensitivity. There is much that still needs improvement. Ours, like most other chalk streams, suffers progressively from the abstractor's pumps, changing agricultural policies and climate. We can only hope that, in the future, wise counsels prevail and that Abbotts Barton can be protected against the negative elements of a changing world.

Despite the many changes that have overtaken the little oasis, so dear to G.E.M.S., most of the locations to which he referred, so nicely illustrated by Jardine, still exist. The "haunt of the aunt sallies" and its tussocks in the Park stream alongside "Ducks' Nest Spinney" even now shelters its aunt sallies. The duns still sail under the poplars along Five-hatches. Bright little trout still flash at the nymphs in the Highland Burn where, at its head below the sluice, the old man caught the trout whose mouths were stuffed with "pea-green" nymphs giving him the "germ of an idea" back in the old Queen's day. Along the main Itchen many of his favourite casts are much as they were. The trout still favour the banks and can take down the spinners of early evening with the merest "sip" and tiniest ring. Abbotts Barton is, even now, "intimate and homely". It is an oasis in the shadow of modern Winchester where, on tranquil summer evenings, the air will fill with clouds of golden needles as the sherry spinners dance in the rays of a tiring sun. The roebuck softly barks and the meadows give up their ghosts. It is on such evenings that the fisherman's hand is always in; his fly frequently finds the tiny dimples and his rod arches to the objections of a powerful trout.

Roy Darlington

Contents

Foreword

——◀◎▶——

WHEN MY brother, G.E.M. Skues, retired from practice as a solicitor in 1940, at the age of 82, he had given up his rod on the Abbotts Barton length of the Itchen just above Winchester and had taken a rod on the Nadder, near Wilton, a few miles from Salisbury. He had long intended to buy or lease a cottage with a small stretch of trout water, but nothing suitable had offered. So, as a temporary measure, he moved to a small hotel close to the Nadder just above Wilton. By this time, with a major war on, neither cottages nor rooms were to be had, so he remained at the hotel until it closed in 1948.

There, when he was not by the waterside, he spent much of his time in a voluminous correspondence with friends from all over the world, in writing reminiscences and articles for the Angling Press and in tying trout flies.

Having fished the Itchen since he was a scholar of Winchester College, he felt very deeply at having to give up his rod on that river. In his book *Sidelines, Sidelights and Reflections* he quoted Kipling's verse:

> Go softly by that river side
>   Or when you would depart,
> You'll find its every winding tied
>   And knotted round your heart.

There is no doubt that that was very true of the Itchen in his case. This book of memories is the outcome.

Most of the material appears now for the first time, but I am indebted to the following for permission to republish articles which had previously appeared in their journals: the Anglers' Club of New York, the Flyfishers' Club, and to the editors of *The Fishing Gazette* and *Angling*.

This is not an angling book in the sense that it sets out to instruct anglers. It does not; but I submit that in its pages anglers will find much useful information, especially in the matter of observation. Many writers on angling urge their readers to observe. The trouble is that most of us observe much without learning anything from it. My brother began like that, and it took him many years to develop that keen power of observation that made him such a master.

C.A.M. Skues

Artist's Foreword

————◄o►————

IN ILLUSTRATING this book, the last to come from the pen of the late G.E.M. Skues, I have endeavoured to provide a pictorial backcloth to the author's words—to capture the charm of the water meadows and the haunts he knew and loved so well.

The river and the meadows have changed little with the passing years. The hut, "PISCATORIBUS SACRUM", has gone, but the old willows remain and "Ducks' Nest Spinney" looks much as it must have done to Skues in the early days of the century. The long stretch above "McCaskie's Corner" flows as clearly as ever beneath the elms and alders, and the evening bells of Winchester Cathedral continue to call across meadows golden with marsh-marigolds and perfumed with crushed watermint. So little has changed. The "olive blues" were hatching at the time of my last visit, plovers wheeled in bewildering gyrations above their nests, and mallard rose in pairs from the sedges. Even old Mullins, the keeper, was apparently ageless; he was as nimble as a man half his three-score-years-and-ten, and with a far brighter eye. Indeed, it was difficult to realise that those spacious days, when speed was not the keynote and dinner with an old Burgundy worthy of the occasion was the accepted climax to the evening rise, had gone.

It is this unchanging background which I have endeavoured to portray and, in doing so, to reveal something of the personality of the Abbotts Barton water. For, like human beings, rivers have their own subtle individualities which we subconsciously note rather than actively perceive. Beyond that, I have tried to depict something of the scenes which the author describes so well; of blue June days and evening rises beneath apricot skies, of leviathan trout that lay "fly replete in depth of June, dawdling away their watery noon", but which in the end were no match for the old man's cunning. If I have captured something of the intangible beauty of the river Skues will one day come to personify, I shall be well content.

ALEX JARDINE
WHITSTABLE.

Full-page Illustrations

———⟨o⟩———

Posthumous Preface
To Join the Brimming River

IF EVER the ensuing collection of my angling papers sees the light in book form it will be after I am under the turf.

Though I do not regret having published *Minor Tactics of the Chalk Stream* (1910, with later editions and other reprints 1914–1924) and *The Way of a Trout with a Fly* (1921, with reprints 1927–1935 and 1949), yet I must own that a reperusal of these books for the purposes of the later reprints has shown me that in some respects my views and practice have matured and that opinions and suggestions which I have disclosed with some confidence in those volumes would have had some modifications had I been publishing them at the time of writing this.

I do not mean that I am in the least repentant of my effort to restore the wet fly to its rightful place on chalk streams. Nor do I doubt that often the sunk fly will still be taken by subaqueously feeding trout. But a long course of experiment with representations of the natural nymph, as accurate in suggestion as my fly-dressing capacity will admit, has convinced me that better results may be obtained on chalk streams with such representations than with the winged or hackled artificial fly. I say advisedly *such* representations, for, speaking generally, the nymphs which the tackle dealer plants on the uninstructed angler are of the most deplorable character—and I am afraid it will be many years before the education of the dealer has progressed far enough to enable him to turn out patterns which, laid side by side with the natural nymph floating in a white dish or baby plate, might look fit to tempt an experienced trout by their verisimilitude.

To my friend the late Col. E.W. Harding, both through his book *The Fly Fisher and the Trout's Point of View,* and through our prolonged correspondence which preceded and followed it, I owe much of the maturing of my views on nymph fishing. In particular, his demonstration that a trout poised under a comparatively smooth surface, looking forwards and upwards, is able to see in reflected panorama in the area of total reflection all that is going on under water for a measurable distance in front of him and that to rise and meet the oncoming nymph just as it arrives at the surface on its way to hatch is his easiest method of securing his prey (while it made me writhe with my own stupidity in not having discovered these vital facts for myself by the sheer light of common sense) led me to close observation of the rises of trout under banks and convinced me that the bulk of these rises, even though they might be marked by bubbles, were not due to the taking of the floating insects but to the absorption of the hatching nymph at the surface—a conclusion reinforced by the constant examinations of the contents of my quarry by means of a marrow scoop and a white enamel cup by the water side, or a baby plate when the representation of the nymphs disclosed was to be attempted at leisure.

For several years past, therefore, I have only fished the floating fly when I was definitely convinced that that was what the trout were taking, and at other times I have used such nymph patterns as the hatching species of sub-imagines suggested (assisting my judgment by the size of the ring, the violence or otherwise and general nature of the trout's movement in taking the nymph), until the capture of a fish enabled me to test my judgment by extracting its contents with the marrow scoop and washing them out into a white cup.

As a consequence, I have dressed a number of nymph patterns, which in dimensions, shape and general coloration have seemed to me to be satisfactory, and on the days when their prototypes were being taken have proved so. Eleven of these were published first in the *Journal of the Flyfishers' Club* and, subsequently, in my book *Sidelines, Sidelights and Reflections*. A further two were published in a later issue of the *Journal of the Flyfishers' Club*. There is therefore no necessity to give details of them again here. I may say, however, that I have not found it necessary in these patterns to go to the labour of representing the wing cases by means of feather as described in *The Way of a Trout* ... and that it is sufficient to suggest the wing cases by a small pad of fur of appropriate colour when wet, with the hackle wound in front.

Apart from these matters, relatively important though they are, it is, I think, rather remarkable that I have so little to repent of or to revise in my two volumes above referred to.

It is, too, a pity that so few trout-fly anglers dress their own flies against the natural insect. It is really much easier in every respect to dress an artificial nymph against the natural nymph floated in any baby plate than to dress an upwinged dun or spinner against the living or newly dead natural insect. Exact measurements of size and proportion can be made and the finished artificial can be put wet under water alongside its prototype for comparison. I am afraid that until a good proportion of anglers dress their own nymphs from the natural insect the tackle dealer will inflict on the public beetles with tails, nymphs of the Professor and of the Bloody Butcher type and suchlike horrors. It is that sort of thing and that only which at times has given me qualms as to the wisdom of my propaganda.

There is, thank heaven, one amateur angler and fly dresser who does not sin against the light. I refer to A. Drewett Chaytor (one of the sons to whom the famous *Letters to a Salmon Fisher's Sons* were addressed), whose dressings of nymphs, as a result of his own experiments (and Captain John D. Evans of Brecon is close up to him), are a delight to see. And here let me add that I have not referred to the patterns which I have myself evolved as pretending to be standards. I would like each angler to produce his own patterns from nature, passing on each successful effort to other fly dressers, to stimulate their further efforts towards perfection.

For myself, by the time, when, if ever, these pages reach the public, my bolt will have been shot and I shall have no more to communicate to my brothers of the fly rod. . . .

Well there it is. *Ave atque vale.*

A Fair Catch?

S OMEWHERE IN the later eighties of last century I was fishing the Itchen with an 11-ft. split cane—a Hardy called the Test rod— on a September afternoon, and was walking down the left bank of the Hog-side stream to get the benefit of the crosswind at the next bend, when a trout rose directly below me, a longish cast downstream. Without waiting to change my fly, I made a cast which pitched it 5 or 6 ft. above him and let it drift down to him. Somewhat to my surprise, he took the fly—but I tightened and had him on. He turned at once and raced downstream, with me in pursuit travelling as fast as I could consistently with winding in rapidly and shortening the line between the fish and my ring. Before I reached the bend I had caught up with him and had him on a short line straight under the arch of my rod and quite close to the bank. He was still full of fight close under my bank, when, to my disgust, my rod straightened as the fish kicked off. But in doing so he lost his balance and for a fraction of a second wallowed belly upwards within reach, then I thrust the net under him and whipped him out on to the bank before he could recover. He was a nice fish somewhere about 1¾ lb. I had knocked him on the head before I had time to consider the question: ought I to have put him back?— a question that has often recurred to me when I have recalled the incident. I felt, however, that I had risen the fish fairly, had hooked him fairly and had played him to a spot within reach of my rod, as was proved by my having netted him while off his balance; the only difference between his position and what it would have been if he had not kicked free was that the hook was no longer in his jaw. What is the verdict?

On another occasion, many years later, on the main stream of Itchen, during a hatch of black gnats, I had mounted a black gnat dressed on two short shanked hooks tied to gut like the late E.M. Tod's Greenwell's Glory double. With it I cast several times to a trout which rose upstream of me to something tiny. Presently, when withdrawing my line to cast again, I became aware of a stout resistance. Supposing that the trout had taken my double deep, I played him downstream some way and eventually netted him out, when I discovered that the fly in his mouth was not my black gnat but a red spinner at the taper end of a rather coarse piece of gut, which in turn was hooked on to a short piece of casting line, obviously broken off either in the strike or in subsequent playing—and this piece had jammed between the two hooks of my double black gnat. That trout, relieved of his attachment, went free. Again—what is the verdict?

Two Blank Days

—————◄O►—————

NOT A very interesting subject? Perhaps not. But if you feel like that about it, pass on. I found it a bit intriguing. I could not fix the date of either of these two days with any exactitude— not even the years.

The first, however, could not have been earlier than 1887, for I recall that I was using a 10-ft. Greenheart of Farlow's, painted a heron blue, which had been presented to me by a client of my firm in that year. It must also have been after 1888 (probably several years after), as I only began fly dressing in that year and I was casting a little red sedge tied with a rolled landrail wing of which I did not discover the merit in my first year or two of fly dressing.

On the occasion in question I had been on the Itchen above Winchester all day without seeing any hatch of fly or rising trout either on the main or the side stream, and seven o'clock found me on the right bank of a straight stretch of a length of the side stream. I resolved to try a few chance casts with one of my little red sedges before going back to my lodging; regardless of the non-existence of any hatch of fly or rise of trout, and as a beginning, I cast over my bank so that the fly only, with about 18 in. of gut, lit on the water. Almost as it lit the fly was grabbed by a trout, which I turned down and promptly netted out, and, as it was under the 12-in. limit of those days on that water, it went back into the river a few steps behind my stance. I dried my fly and made a fresh cast close to the bank a few feet higher upstream. That, too, was taken, but again by a trout below the 12-in. limit, which in due course I returned to the water downstream. Cast after cast in the 200 yds. or so up to the Cow Bridge (which crossed the stream about its middle), all delivered close to the bank, elicited rise after rise of trout, all of which took firmly, and all of which, being below the size limit, were promptly returned to the river, so that by the time I came within casting distance of the Cow Bridge I had had out and returned no fewer than nineteen unsizeable trout. The bridge, however, presented a more hopeful prospect, for past experience had led me to hope for much better fish on the far side of the span. Not a bit of it. The fly was grabbed as promptly as ever, but again the trout proved unsuitable. So, after turning him in again, I reeled up in disgust and took the path across the meadow to return to my lodging to record a blank day.

The second occasion I have to record occurred some years later—a bright, fresh, hopeful sort of midsummer's day. Yet hour by hour went by without any hatch of fly or any sign on the surface to tempt me to cast, and by five o'clock I had got to the corner of the first bend below the railway arch. That corner usually held two or three decent trout, and I approached it cautiously so as not to scare them. There was no rise there, however, and after waiting a few minutes I dropped my fly—a red spinner with a claret seal's fur body and a sharp blue cock's hackle—at the point where I had hoped to find a takable fish. At the second or third offer it was firmly grabbed—but by a trout of disappointing size, which had to go back. Two or three more took the fly below the railway arch—but again were unsizeable. So I turned to the side stream which at this point approached the main. Here again trout after trout (though here they *were* rising) took my red spinner gaily and had to go back for the same unsatisfactory reason, until I had brought the number caught and returned to twenty-four, and then, in despair, I reeled up and went in to record another blank day. In Norway, Bavaria, Württemberg and Normandy I have caught over twelve brace in a day, but never had to record a blank.

Now why on both these occasions were only unsizeable fish willing to feed?

Tale of a Gibe

JUST RECENTLY I have had to submit (quite good-temperedly, of
course) to having my leg pulled by a distinguished American
angler who was fishing the Itchen as my guest on a date in an early
year of the present century—I may at once admit that I exposed
myself to the gibe by my ignorance at the time of a fact which
subsequent experiences on that none-too-easy water drove home.
Here is the tale.

We entered the meadows from the west by a path across the
fields, which took us first to the side stream at a point two or three
hundred yards below the shallow illustrated by Dr. Barton on the
photo reproduced as a frontispiece to my third book *Sidelines,
Sidelights and Reflections*. Whether we began at the city bathing
place or at the long spinney upstream of it I cannot recall. But it
was not long before we reached the deepish stretch of the side
stream which is known on the estate map as the Black Ditch and
were downstream of a cross-drain which carried water westward
across the meadows.

There I pointed out to our American friend (A.F. hereafter for
brevity) a jutting point behind which there had sheltered through
the season a biggish and highly wary trout which had caused tribu-
lation and disappointment to various anglers. A.F. prepared to cast
for him, first showing me his fly, a big one of the sedge type. I

confess I had no belief in a fly of such a size in the daytime and I recommended A.F. to try something more modest than a Surrey fowl. He persisted, however, in giving it a trial, and it was not long before a hefty neb broke the ruffled surface at the point I had indicated, simultaneously absorbing A.F.'s Surrey fowl, and, after the usual argument, was persuaded to come ashore with the rest of his 36 oz. A.F. was naturally pleased at this vindication of his better judgment, especially as he was quite new to the water and I had been fishing it since 1883; yet I doubt—I doubt gravely—whether A.F. realised any more than I did that it was the special conditions of that *place and day* which accounted for his success—for the Surrey fowl, tried in several places during that day, had no more triumphs over our Itchen fish. It took me years and several experiences to get at what I believe to have been the true solution of the puzzle.

Experiment 1. A stretch running west and east from McCaskie's Corner, a violent wind from the south with a strong ruffle under the left bank—a good fish breaking the surface once in the ruffle under the left bank, and a second time to absorb a biggish fly of the March brown type. Weight 2 lb. 13 oz.

Experiment 2. A wind, far too violent to cast into, blowing straight down the stretch of the main river below the luncheon hut—a sedge fly on a No. 3 hook, which overnight had been responsible for several trout which were taking young toads, had been left on and was cast tentatively to a place under the far bank which a good trout was known to frequent; the immediate acceptance of the fly on its being dropped in the ruffle on the trout's corner. Weight 2 lb. 12 oz. A few yards downstream another 2 lb. 6 oz.

Experiment 3. An early evening, which, far from being still, was ruffled by a strong downstream wind at a point near McCaskie's Corner where the river turned left. A three-pounder known to haunt the spot. Tender of a large sedge fly on a No. 4 hook; demise of three-pounder.

There were other cases more or less in point, but they were capped by:

Experiment 4. A schoolboy from Winchester College, who had no fishing experience and did not know that a trout lay under the footbridge which crossed the side stream by the luncheon hut and scarcely deigned to move when one crossed the plank bridge, came as guest of a member and flapped a big fly under the plank and scored the only four-pounder that had been taken on the fly from the fishery in all the years I had known it.

Deduction: A big fly in a gale producing a ruffle over the haunt of a big trout is apt to be fatal to the big trout.

Now did A.F. know that?

P.D.Q.

————◄○►————

I T WAS on an August Bank Holiday, somewhere between the two
wars. I had gone down to Winchester from London overnight to
keep an appointment with the rector of Martyr Worthy (some four
miles along the road which runs along the west side of the Itchen
to Alresford) to settle a little matter connected with a marriage
settlement of which we were co-trustees, and soon after nine
o'clock in the morning I set out to visit him. For some reason
which I do not recall no bus was available, and I made up my mind
to pad the hoof. Unfortunately, by the time I had covered the first
mile of my journey the new shoes I was wearing had proved to be
a tight fit and I was limping painfully, but I felt I had gone too far
to turn back though it promised to be a roasting day. But after I had
covered a few hundred yards more a car came up behind me, driven
by a good Samaritan, who stopped to inquire where I was going
and could he give me a lift. I told him my destination, and he
replied, "Why, that's my father—hop in." A few minutes later he
delivered me at the rectory. But as he did so, he inquired when I
wanted to go back, adding, "I shall be driving back to Winchester
at eleven-fifteen and would be glad to take you if you could wait
till then."

My business with the rector did not take long. The son was as
good as his word, and by half-past eleven had dropped me within

a few steps of the keeper's cottage where I kept my rod and gear. Having secured these, and having exchanged my uncomfortable shoes for a pair of easy rubber Wellingtons, I made speed across the city park to the south-east corner, where a man who lets out boats to citizens who wish to paddle on the side stream between his corner and the city bathing place was to be found and got him to put me across to the narrow strip of land dividing the side stream of the Itchen from an offshoot, romantically called Swift Lake—being neither swift nor a lake. A few minutes' walk upstream brought me to a bridge, which was but a few steps from McCaskie's Corner in the main river where it turns sharply from south to east, and by noon I had my rod up, my line through the rings, my cast (already damped) lengthened by 16 or 18 in. of 4X gut point knotted on, and I had only to put on a fly to be ready to begin.

McCaskie's Corner is usually a safe find for a good fish or two, but, this being Bank Holiday, the opposite bank for 100 yds. downriver was crowded with trespassing bathers, and others swimming in the stream had made fishing at that point impossible. Fortunately these activities did not extend round the bend, so I started to watch the surface upstream of the corner. Nothing was doing under the banks, but it was not long before I espied high in the water a dark shape about half-way to mid-stream, and saw it turn sharply to the left, open its mouth and take something without breaking the surface.

Experience of previous years had taught me that a tiny nymph dressed on a tiny sneckbend to the pattern No. XI in *Nymph Fishing for Chalk Stream Trout* was at times as good in August as in April and May, so I lost no time in tying one on and dropping it out a foot or so to the left side of the trout. He turned to it, and as I saw his mouth close I tightened and presently escorted him ashore.

KINGSWORTHY POST OFFICE

Again and again, in the 300 or 400 yds. to the next bend of the main river, was this experience repeated, each fish being plainly visible just under the surface, and by the time the cathedral clock chimed one I had collected five nice trout, all sizeable, though none quite 2 lb., without a loss and all on the unchanged nymph.

When I got on the water at noon I had thought that on such a blazing day I should be indeed lucky if I escaped a blank, and here was I an hour later with five nice unexpected trout in my bag—reflecting that if I went on fishing I could only take one more to have got my limit and should either have to go up to town on a later train, packed to the back teeth, or stay the night in Winchester and go up next morning in a train even more crowded. Calculating that if I made a run for it I might just catch an early afternoon train for town, I crossed the side stream by the footbridge, raced to the keeper's, left rod and gear in his charge, got to my hotel in the City Road, lunched and caught the three-seventeen train with my two and a half brace.

My only regret was that I could not give the fish, the whole five of them, to the good Samaritan, but I had been afraid to ask his address or to give or imply a promise of trout, for, as surely as I did so, I *knew* I should score a blank—especially on such a roasting August day. Still, it appeared to me that the whole performance might fairly be said to have been P.D.Q.

Trackless Drag

———◄o►———

IT WAS a roasting Saturday afternoon in July, late in the last decade of the nineteenth century. I had come down from London in the morning expecting to be alone, and had found that my host, who had kindly given me a season ticket, was on the water with a couple of guests. Such remnants of good manners as I had surviving from my public school and the teachings of an admirable mother indicated that in these circumstances it would be well to confine my activities to the short stretch of meadow bounding the side stream for a couple of hundred yards or so above the Ducks' Nest Spinney. The river there was far from full. It was, in fact, slow, and dead smooth, being sheltered from the very faint westerly drift of air—one could not call it a breeze—by the long extension of the north end of the spinney, for the entire length of the meadow.

Things did not look hopeful. There seemed to be no hatch of fly and no trout in sight. But presently, when I had run my line through the rings and looped my cast to it and had gone slowly up the entire length of the meadow and started down again, I became aware of a very thin trickle of pale watery duns drifting slowly under the eastern bank, and at length descried a trout. Two or three pale wateries drifted over him unregarded. But presently one of them rose from the surface and dropped on it again in a sort of hop just behind the trout's eye. The trout tilted its neb slowly and sucked in the fly. That gave me a clue.

Not long before, I had acquired the only skin of a dotterel that I ever in my life possessed. I had tied on beautiful 22-in. lengths of fresh gossamer gut supplied by George Holland some three or four hackled flies to the following prescription:

Hook	OO round bend
Tying silk	Yellow
Hackle	Pale dotterel—three close turns on edge.

Of these, I had two in soak in my damper, and I knotted one to the end of my cast, and carefully dried the hackle before casting. On putting it across under the far bank—a nice easy cast—I found it floated beautifully on the tips of the hackle fibres, and I eased it over the trout. It was ignored— so were several more natural flies on several successive casts—each delivered with a careful avoidance of drag. So I looked for and presently found another trout, hovering languidly near the surface under the far bank. Him, too, I covered several times perfectly without a particle of drag till the fly was well below the fish. But at last I made a rather careless cast, which lit well above the trout, and, to my dismay, began to drag just as the fly was about to reach the fish and to draw the fly away almost at right angles to the far bank, but, curiously enough, without crinkling the surface film. Imagine my surprise when I saw the trout turn aside, follow the retreating fly and, softly sucking it in, turn back to resume his station. This, however, he was not allowed to do and presently was wrapped in a napkin and put in my bag.

The hint was not lost on me, and before I went in for dinner four more trout had been lured by the dragging fly, which made no mark on the surface, and joined number one in my bag. I could not find any more, so I reeled up and went in, well content with about 7 lb. of fish. Incidentally, these five were the only trout taken that day on my host's two miles or more of water.

Tup's Indispensable

––––––◀◦▶––––––

THE *Field* of 25th May 1901 contained in it the late Humphrey Priddis's Itchen report for the previous week, over the then well-known pseudonym "Dabchick", an account of a rod having killed three brace of trout and returned four brace on the preceding Saturday on Tup's Indispensable. The editor was assailed by numerous inquiries for the pattern and its makers. In the meantime, I, as the angler in question, had communicated an account of the fly and its virtues to the *Fishing Gazette*, where it appeared on 6th July 1901. The dressing having been communicated to me (and I believe also to the late C.A. Hassam) in confidence by Mr. R. Austin of Tiverton, the inventor, remained a secret till his death and for many years afterwards until his daughter gave up fly fishing and assented to publication of the prescription. In the meantime, many attempts to reproduce the pattern had been made, and though probably some of them caught an occasional trout, the original dressing in the hands of Mr. Austin and his daughter retained its supremacy to the last. Poor Mr. Austin got tired of dressing the hundreds of dozens ordered of him. He told me that a Dorsetshire customer complained to him that the Frome "stank" of T.I. from Maiden Newton to the sea.

I confess that I took the liberty of applying the essential principles of Mr. Austin's pattern to a number of variations and with success.

––––––––––––––––––––– ⚜ 44 ⚜ –––––––––––––––––––––

On the occasion reported in the *Field* on 25th May 1901 my fishing was confined to a stretch of the Abbotts Barton length of the Itchen between the spinney upstream of the railway and the small stream which joins the two branches of the river, less than 100 yds. in all, and my seven brace were collected from under the left bank, fishing across from the right bank.

I propose now to tell of another seven brace taken on T.I. lower down, and twelve years or so later.

The publication in March 1910 of my first book, *Minor Tactics of the Chalk Stream*, led at long last, through the intervention of a relative, to my acquaintance and subsequent friendship with L.B., a brilliant angler who was also a distinguished landscape painter—subsequently successively A.R.A. and R.A., and in the spring of 1917 he came down to Winchester to share a rod with me for a day on the Itchen.

For some reason, probably the presence on the main stream of other members of the syndicate, we found ourselves limited to the side stream, beginning just above the Ducks' Nest Spinney and fishing from the right bank. There was a brisk breeze from the north, which was rather too much for my damaged right wrist, but L.B. made nothing of it and found no difficulty in covering trout after trout with the T.I. which I had supplied. So we arranged that he should fish out the straight above the spinney, after which I was to take the next stretch, which came in from the east so that I would have the wind to help me, while L. B. busied himself with his canvas and easel.

The way in which he was putting his fly to fish after fish in spite of the breeze was masterly, and the T.I. seemed entirely to the taste of the trout, so that by the time he had reached the bend he had collected four brace of quite nice fish. And after lunch he retired to his easel and palette with complete content.

The trout lying under the left bank in the length left to me were still amenable to the T.I., but not quite so eager; and by the time I covered the middle of the stretch I had only two and a half brace, when, near the top of the length, there leaped into the air a trout which I estimated at 2¾ lb. I moved up at once to fish for him and did my best for a good half-hour, without, however, provoking the least response. So I turned down to rejoin L.B. in the meadows, where he had pitched his easel. This involved, after I had passed through the Ducks' Nest Spinney, the crossing by plank of a field drain which ran from the bottom of the shallow in the side stream due west for some way across the meadow. But as I approached the plank I became aware of something I had never seen there either before or since. Right under the plank a good trout was rising, feeding busily. I dare not cast upstream of the plank, firstly because of the drag, which would have been inevitable, but also for fear that if I hooked the trout he would dash downstream and smash me inevitably. The only thing to do was to try to get T.I. to the fish under the plank—something almost impossible. Yet after a number of shots the impossible came off. The fly lit right under the plank to the left of the trout, who turned and sucked it in greedily, and then raced, soundly hooked, for the tail of the shallows of the side stream. I lost no time in passing my rod, top foremost, under the plank, then running to the point of exit of the drain and getting my drowned line into the air. The trout had made off down the side stream at a point where it was heavily weeded—but he must have made more mistakes than I did, for I presently succeeded in getting him up under my own bank and netting him out. He weighed 2 lb. 3 oz. and made up our joint seven brace for the day.

Incidentally, during the next week-end I was able to verify my guess of the weight of the trout that leapt. He was exactly 2¾ lb. and took my T.I. at the point whence I had seen him leap.

Zeiss Glass

———◀◦▶———

Y EARS AGO Dr. E.A. Barton (it must have been after 1916 when
I made his acquaintance), for some reason which I cannot
account for, unless it were the innate generosity of his heart,
presented me with a little monocular Zeiss glass, which in repose
stood about one inch high and which had to be adjusted to one's
vision by pulling out the lower lens. So adjusted it would enable
one to spot every detail of a fly on a leaf at a distance of 30, 40 or
even 50 yds. But it had the further capacity of enabling one to spot,
under water, at 30 yds. or under, the position and movements of
trout which were not readily to be detected by the naked eye. This
power was specially valuable in the period (often prolonged)
preceding the hatch of fly when trout were taking up position deep
under banks in anticipation of the ascent of nymphs to the
surface—and it was not long before I was putting this power to the
proof. Where the water was deep under the banks it was necessary
to ensure the ready sinking of the nymph and the cast to attract the
attention of the trout to the nymph, having first used the little Zeiss
glass to detect the presence of a waiting trout. Then at times it was
possible to glimpse, as the floating part of the line went by, the shift-
ing across the gravel of a shadow, which was in fact a trout, and its
turning back to the far bank, at which one instinctively tightened
and found a good trout was fast. For such fishing naturally a sunny

THE KEEPER'S COTTAGE

day with little wind presented advantages, and a bottom of light gravel was easier than a muddy or weedy one to work on.

I remember the first day I used the glass—a May day with a light easterly breeze and a pleasant amount of sun. I took the left bank of a length that ran for about 300 yds. north to south. So I had both sun and what little wind there was at my back. There was no sign of any hatch of fly or rise of fish when I arrived, and I walked slowly up 100 yds. of the right bank without seeing any movement. All that 100 yds. of the right bank was overhung with big tussocks under which the river ran to 6 or 8 ft. deep over a margin of yellow marsh. Then it occurred to me that I was neglecting an opportunity to test Dr. Barton's gift, and I returned to my starting point and began to re-examine the run beneath the tussocks with the aid of the little Zeiss glass. I was surprised to see how it seemed to clarify the water under the tussocks, and presently I discovered something lying deep, which might be a trout. It was, and after my nymph had been down across his post several times he rose in the water and turned down again. But the hook was in his mouth. I do not recall all the detail of the ensuing two hours during which I worked slowly up to the top-most row of tussocks but it grew increasingly sunny, and, though no rise broke the surface, there were two brace of nice trout in my bag, all on nymph fished deep.

Then the sun came out quite hot—there ensued a very sudden and active hatch of black gnats, which brought the trout to the surface. I had some difficulty in finding an attractive pattern of fly, but I was able before the rise was over to make up my limit without any further aid from the doctor's gift.

A First-Rate Rod

◄○►

EARLY IN the second decade of the present century a sister of mine took a holiday from headmistress-ship and spent it in the tiny community of Lamorna near Penzance, thus coming into touch with T.J. Lamorna Birch, who not long afterwards became an R.A. In March 1910 my first angling book, *Minor Tactics of the Chalk Stream*, was published. It seems to have made an impression on the artist, for, having made my sister's acquaintance, he expressed, through her, his wish to meet me and offered to present one of his charming landscapes, a view of his dwelling in Lamorna with a brook, in which he frequently cast a successful fly, running towards the observer. In due course this led not only to a meeting between us but to the artist becoming my Itchen guest for the opening day of a season. He came equipped not only with rod and tackle but also with easel and painting equipment. We began on the side stream at the Ducks' Nest Spinney, just above the point illustrated in my third book, *Sidelines, Sidelights and Reflections*, over the title "The Haunt of the Aunt Sallies". Birch's rod was, like my own, a Leonard, but a ten-footer against my nine-footer and definitely more powerful. The wind was blowing stiffly but not intolerably downstream, and I was immensely impressed by the straightness of the line he drove into it and by the accuracy of his casting. The wind was too much for my little nine-footer, so I stayed behind Birch as he worked slowly up to the corner where the stream turned south from a stretch which ran east to west. I had imagined that Birch would have gone on fishing round the bend, but he wanted to get back to his painting gear and was content with the basket of four brace which he had collected. So I began at the corner and went on fishing the east-to-west length. As I was doing so, I saw a big fish spring 2 ft. out of the water under the south bank near the top of the stretch. I did not, however, hurry to reach the spot, and collected several fish on the way (I have no record of the precise number, but they were enough to content me), though I could not bring up the big fish I had seen jump.

By the evening, when it was time to go in, I went down to rejoin Birch at his easel.

Thereafter for many years Birch was my guest on the Itchen each spring either just before or just after the opening of the Royal Academy, and more and more impressed me with the quality of his fishing, ranking with two other friends of mine as unsurpassed by any other rods I ever saw at work either on that or any other water.

Those were the days before any limits on baskets were imposed.

Three in One

————◀○▶————

IT WAS a bright July morning in the days when I was a comparative beginner. I was walking downstream towards the Five Hatches, with the side stream on my left and a sharp little channel two feet or more deep on my right, running brimful of shining water collected from the tables on its far side. My attention had been mainly on the side stream in the hope of finding a rising trout and getting below him without putting him down. But a sort of pleasant chuckle in the narrow channel to my right, seeming to suggest that water from the side stream was somehow breaking through the bank into that channel, attracted my attention. Cautiously I peeped over, and through the overhanging grasses I espied three quite sizeable trout frantically busy, apparently wolfing minnows at the point where the water from the side stream was coming through. Quickly I got my landing net into the water behind the three, and as they shrank back I lifted it, with every one of the three trout in it. Then over to the side stream I turned the three in.

Irwin Cox, the lessee of the water, was down fishing that day and I told him the story. "What did you do?" he asked. "Turned them into the side stream," I said. "Oh," said Mr. Cox, "you should have killed them. I would have. . . ."

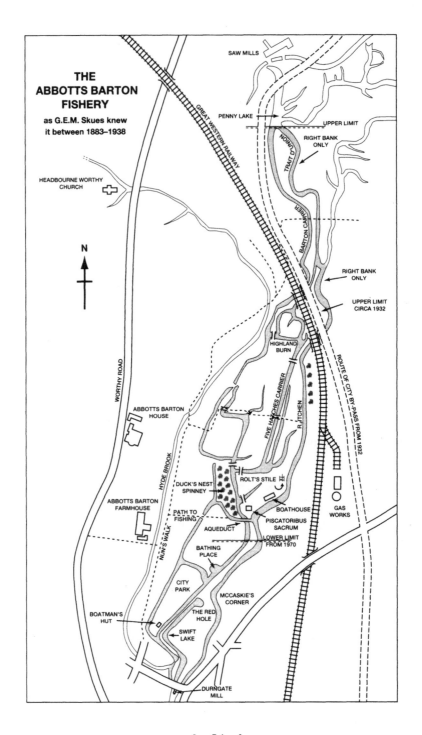

THE
ABBOTTS BARTON
FISHERY

as G.E.M. Skues knew
it between 1883–1938

N

HEADBOURNE WORTHY
CHURCH

SAW MILLS

GREAT WESTERN RAILWAY

PENNY LAKE

UPPER LIMIT

RIGHT BANK
ONLY

TRAIT D'UNION

BARTON CARRIER

RIGHT BANK
ONLY

UPPER LIMIT
CIRCA 1932

ROUTE OF CITY BY-PASS FROM 1932

HIGHLAND
BURN

FIVE HATCHES CARRIER

R. ITCHEN

WORTHY ROAD

ABBOTTS BARTON
HOUSE

HYDE BROOK

DUCK'S NEST
SPINNEY

ROLT'S STILE

BOATHOUSE

GAS
WORKS

ABBOTTS BARTON
FARMHOUSE

PATH TO
FISHING

AQUEDUCT

PISCATORIBUS
SACRUM

LOWER LIMIT
FROM 1970

NUN'S WALK

BATHING
PLACE

CITY
PARK

MCCASKIE'S
CORNER

BOATMAN'S
HUT

THE RED
HOLE

SWIFT
LAKE

DURNGATE
MILL

Two Alders

I BEGAN MY serious trout fishing on the Itchen in May 1883, my previous two seasons, 1875 and 1876, on Old Barge (when I was a boy at Winchester), handicapped with a deplorable rod and an entirely unsuitable line, being counted out—and I did not begin fly dressing until 1887. But not long after that I acquired the third edition (1875) of the Rev. Charles Kingsley's *Prose Idylls* and read with special interest his "Chalk Stream Studies". Yet even then, ignorant as I was, I was unable to accept with faith his enthusiasm for large patterns such as the alder, the caperer and the governor, and large palmers for chalk stream trout, and his contempt for small flies, seeing that none of the anglers I met on that river ever used any but small flies (outside the mayfly season). Besides Francis Francis and W. Senior there were several good anglers among them. Moreover, I noted that the reverend gentleman included in his team of chalkstream flies the March brown (which does not occur in chalk streams) he also recommended "the Turkey brown ephemera" (by which I imagine he meant paralep?) in the submerged stage, though up till then I had never seen that fly taken by a solitary trout (indeed in my fifty-six years' experience of the Itchen I never saw one taken, nor did I ever find one in the contents of a trout's stomach in any one of my hundreds of examinations of the contents of their stomachs).

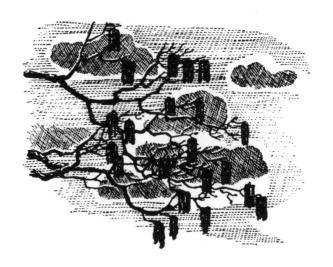

I therefore felt more than doubtful about the use on Itchen of the alder which, though it appeared annually, was always in scanty supply, and I do not think I possessed a sample until after I had paid a visit to Bavaria in 1900, when, impressed by the huge hatches of large sedge flies, I included some large alders in my purchases for a visit to the same river in which I hoped would be the mayfly season of 1904. I then bought of Peeks in the Grays Inn Road, in addition to a number of sedge, a couple of dozen black alders, not exactly of the Kingsley tie, but a pattern, winged with double slips of game hen secondaries, sloped well back over the body and hackled with a black cock's hackle in front of the wings and tied on Hall's Snecky Limerick hooks Nos. 3 and 4. That was a pattern I never saw occasion to change—my fortnight's fishing in Bavaria in 1904 brought me two hundred and sixty-one trout (kept and handed over alive to the riparian owners) in addition to under-sized fish returned. Most fell to the alder; mayfly scarcely appeared. The following year I was again too early for the mayfly, but took two hundred and sixty-five trout in thirteen days mainly on alder. The bushes by the riverside had a plum-coloured haze over them due to alder flies buzzing around them.

Still I saw few alders on the Itchen and none taken; but in 1905 or 1906 I had a Whitsuntide, three days on the Nadder, in which of one hundred and four trout caught eighty-four took alder (same pattern), ten red quill and ten mayfly. All but three and a half brace (these on the last day) went back. So it went on till 1913, when I received (as a consequence of the publication of *Minor Tactics of the Chalk Stream*) an invitation to fish two days mayfly on the Chilton Ffolliot length of the Kennet. I said I would prefer the alder season if that would be agreeable to my host. He kindly accepted the suggestion, and on the first day I caught twenty trout on the same pattern of alder. On the second day my host took me down to his brother's stretch below the Hungerford Town water, where again I caught ten brace by lunch-time. On each occasion I returned the lot.

A year or two later a big trout, estimated at 5 lb., took up his post on a bit of bare chalk under the east bank of the Itchen and was fished by all the members of my syndicate in turn, without his taking the slightest notice. Here, I thought, is an occasion on which the alder might attract. He never turned to look at it. After four or five weeks on the same spot, he was missing and did not return— probably wormed by a poacher. One day, a year or two later, I was crossing the meadow by a path across the middle, which was bounded on the north by a ditch or drain carrying the water collected from the drainage system of the upper meadows and taking it to a point where it passed under the road which I was using to a drain which ran straight for about 250 yds. to join the side stream. There was sometimes a trout or so to be seen in the ditch above-mentioned, but they always looked languid and sick fish, uninterested in food. On this occasion a trout surprised me by rising just above the place where the ditch water passed under the road. I looked over the ditch and saw him cruising about over a small area. So I changed my fly and tied on a black alder and dibbed it carefully on his back. He turned and took it and, after a feeble fight, was transferred to the bag.

A week or two later, walking up the drain below the road, I espied a long yellow fish under the east bank of the drain, and as he seemed interested in food I tied on a biggish red sedge with landrail wings and cast it to him. He followed it up for a yard or two—then returned to position. Twice more this occurred, so I changed the fly, putting on a black alder. The fish looked at it, turned away, then followed it again some way and left it, to return to his position— when suddenly he turned again, rushed downstream and gulped the fly. He was 2 lb. 8 oz.—but flabby and in poor condition, better out than in.

These were the only trout I ever took on an alder on the Itchen—nor did I ever hear of anyone doing better with that fly.

Stimulation

————◄○►————

ONE SUMMER Saturday afternoon in the early 'thirties I was coming in from Itchen side and had reached the Alresford Road, when I became aware of a young Irishman who had served his articles with my junior partner and was now helping a pleasant-looking young woman from a motor drawn up by the roadside. He introduced me, and I suggested that if the lady was interested in fishing he should bring her on the morrow into the water-meadows.

On the following day I had fished all the morning with no effect, when, soon after two o'clock, looking across the river and meadows from the east bank of Itchen, I saw my young friend and his lady entering the meadows from the gate by Abbotts Barton farm. Shocked at having nothing to show them as a result of my morning's toil, I moved rapidly upstream to where my friend, A.D. Chaytor (one of the sons of the great Chaytor, K.C.), had been fishing, to find that he had collected some brace on nymph. With no time to be lost, I began again at the top of my beat near the gasworks and almost immediately was into a good fish which resolutely towed me downstream almost to the bend below Rolt's Stile before I got him into the net. On the way down I saw that my hooked fish had disturbed another good trout which lay under the west bank just above Rolt's Stile. In spite of his recent disturbance, this trout found my nymph too attractive to resist. He was even a better fish than the former one and he only came to net a few yards above the weed rack bridge, which the two young people were approaching, when I netted him. The priest having done its office, I wrapped the fish up in a napkin and was able to provide the young lady with a brace weighing 2 lb. 1 oz. and 2 lb. 13 oz. caught just in time. Should I have caught them but for the stimulus of the coming of that young couple hoping to see some trout? Very likely not.

On the following Saturday afternoon the girl brought her father to look on—they found me on the east bank on the length above the bridge with the weed rack and took back with them another brace that failed to resist the temptations of the artificial nymph.

On the Way to the Nymph

————◄○►————

THERE WAS a place in my progress from wet fly to nymph which I have hitherto not recorded. I think it should be. It came about through my acquiring, almost simultaneously, some small blue steel eyed hooks with sharp points, and a variety of quills, blue and red macaws and others. With these I tied a number of fancy patterns of which the blue macaws with yellow quills, giving bright red whisks, were perhaps the most attractive. In those days we were blessed (if we could have thought so) with upstream neighbours, who seemed to make it a duty to send down upon us each week-end floating rafts of cut river weed, and these anchored against our river banks and after a while one found that the edges of these rafts were patrolled by trout which were not learned enough to realise that these blue macaw bodied things were not real nymphs, with the result that, fishing close to the margin of these rafts, one collected quite a few unsuspecting trout which took these fancy nymphs. But in those days I had not discovered the marrow scoop. When I did—oh, when I did—the edge of weed raft grew even more profitable.

THE MIDDLE STREAM

Re-Stocking

I FEAR I may have acquired a reputation on the Abbotts Barton Syndicate for meanness through my having always voted against expenditure on re-stocking the fishery. In all the years that Mr. Irwin E.A. Cox rented it, from 1885 down to about 1917, and for a year or two longer, that part of the Itchen had always not stocked itself from the reeds on the shallow at the top of the length and above it but had also sent down quantities of trout to stock the city waters below, and it was only when the lack of netting and wood-cutting and mudding during the war years had allowed the pike to increase so much that our stock of trout fell off badly. Yet their quality was so high that I would have been content to leave things to nature and the head of trout to satisfactory dimensions. Well, I was out-voted and I paid up my quota, but the stock which for several years were imported and turned in did us little good. Those caught were too small to be kept and the bait fishers in the "Weirs" (the city waters) caught and killed them in scores.

Later the young stock were confined in a short stretch of ditch-wide running water near the upper end of the fishing, and were fed on horsemeat until big enough to be turned into the main river, but I always hated the idea of feeding up young stock to be killed, as much as I dislike the idea of feeding young pheasants till the end of September and shooting them on 1st October.

Apart from that consideration, I doubt whether the members and their guests got any sport worth counting out of the stock we turned in. I raised my limit to 2 lb. and kept that up till 1924, when things seemed to be returning to normal, and I went back to my 1½-lb. limit.

The re-stocking, however, went on with much the same results—and in that year I kept thirty-five brace of which eight brace exceeded 2 lb. I am therefore quite unrepentant, and, I think, justifiably so.

Three Grayling

<del>◄o►</del>

O NE AUTUMN day during the 1914–18 War I met with my late
friend, Hugh T. Sheringham, and discussed grayling and
grayling flies with him. He, like me, was kindly provided by Mr.
Irwin Cox with a season ticket on the Abbotts Barton stretch of the
Itchen and he told me that in a small length I called the *Trait d'Union*
(because it broke away from the side stream just below Kingsworthy
Mill and in 100 yds. or so joined the main Itchen) he had spotted, but
failed to catch, a small shoal of biggish grayling that occupied a deepish hole a long cast above Cart Bridge, which served the carting of
hay crops from the meadows to the east, and he recommended me to
have a shot at them. The Cart Bridge in question was barred to unau-
thorised passengers by an iron gate some 15 ft. high with a *chevaux
de frise* of spear-pointed spikes radiating in a half circle across the
entire top of the gate and impossible to climb round, and when not
in use the gate was kept studiously locked.

On a sunny Saturday afternoon a few days later I stood by the
west side of the Cart Bridge and studied the bottom of the *Trait
d'Union*—here 5 or 6 ft. in depth, and, sure enough, on the bare
chalky bottom of a deep hole in the centre I espied a small shoal of
three grayling approaching— 2 lb. apiece. I accordingly knotted on
my cast a fly I had prepared experimentally for the occasion. This
was the tie:

Hook	No. 2 Pryce-Tannatt's round bend
Tying silk	Crimson
Hackle	Soft blue (dark) hen
Body	Peacock herl dyed claret.

I had not begun to fish when I became aware of three khaki-clad figures crossing the meadows towards the far side of the iron gate. I called to them that the gate was locked and impassable. Did that stop them? Not much! One after another, like three monkeys, they scaled that fiendish gate—got over the spear spikes at the top (which I would not have attempted for £100) and came down on to the Cart Bridge on my side.

They then waited to see what I was doing, and I pointed out to them the little clutch of three grayling in the deep hole in midstream. They then stood aside to let me cast and looked on for a few minutes, then turned to make their way westward to cross the side stream, when I called, "Any of you like a grayling?" They came rushing back to be first to get a grayling and I was able to net out and hand to the winner a grayling not far from 2 lb. The three then turned and were making off, when I called, "Anyone else like another?" and two came rushing back to get a similar fish out of my landing net.

Before they reached the bridge to the west again, I called, "Who's for number three?" and the third man came back to receive his similar fish. "No good to wait for any more—that's the lot."

As it turned out, it was so, for, though each of these three fish took the fly directly it was offered, not another fish did I get that afternoon.

The Germ of an Idea

---◀○▶---

I N 1938, in the course of turning over what I had kept of over
fifty years of angling correspondence, I came across some letters
which brought back to my mind that in the 'eighties of last century
I was already intrigued by the idea of representing the nymph arti-
ficially. In the spring of 1888 (Whitsuntide in all probability) I had
a Saturday and Monday on the Itchen, and on the Saturday, fishing
up a straight stretch known as the Highland Burn, which left the
west branch of the Itchen through a large sluice and ran straight
across the meadows almost to the east main branch near the railway
arch before turning south, I put my pink wickham on to the rush
of water from the sluice and, rising a trout, struck too hard and left
in him my fly and two strands of the gossamer's gut, then unwisely
used. On the Monday, casting the same pattern to the same spot, I
hooked and landed a very pretty trout a trifle over 1 lb. in weight
(takable in those days) from which I recovered the pink wickham
and the two strands of gut I had lost on the Saturday, but in extracting the recovered fly I found that the mouth of the fish was dotted
with a number of tiny pea-green creatures, which I later learnt were
nymphs.

Not long before this incident I had read in the *Fishing Gazette*
a letter from a correspondent in which the writer had jeered at
the credulity of anglers who imagined that trout fed on natural

flies. I had not known what he meant, but I suppose that these little green creatures supplied the answer. In September 1888 I had a week on the Coquet, in one afternoon of which I caught in one spot thirty-eight trout on a small sherry-coloured spinner tied with a body of flat tawny gut dyed a deep orange which I had dressed to represent a natural fly I had caught the previous day. During that visit I also had several nice trout fishing the evening rise with a representation of the spinner of the August dun, also tied with a body of flat tawny gut dyed a very hot orange. So when I got home I wrote to George Holland, who had then leapt into celebrity as a fly dresser, and I suggested the practicability of imitating larvae of duns with dyed gut wound wet over a bare hook. In reply he wrote me, under date 15th October 1888, "Larvae have been tied years ago by Mr. Marryat and myself, though not with gut as you suggest, which might be an improvement. They never killed any fish either with larvae or shrimp which I enclose. (Please return them as I keep them for curiosities.)"

Some time subsequently I wrote him suggesting the use of sponge for representing nymphs. He commented in his reply on my having unusual ideas, but apparently did not pursue the matter, and for a long time, discouraged no doubt by the failure of G. S. Marryat and Holland, neither did I.

I propounded the same idea in 1889 to Mr. Austin of Tiverton, the inventor of Tup's Indispensable. He tied flies with gut bodies with no great success, but on 12th June 1889 he wrote me, "It occurs to me that there is a lot of larva that might be imitated in summer with advantage." But I never heard of his making anything of the idea.

It was years later before I made much of a move to represent the larvae of nymph.

THE GATEWAY FROM THE KEEPER'S COTTAGE

I got an idea, however, from weed cutting which was not entirely unreliable. When weed cutting had taken place, rafts of weed, sometimes of considerable length, would anchor themselves along the banks, and I found at times that trout, whether they were rising on these edges or not, would often take a landrail and hare's ear sedge drifted close to the edge of a raft anchored to the far bank.

Then I became possessed of some blue macaw feathers and was tempted to tie some weird-looking nymphs by winding a strand—yellow with a dark blue rib—on a small hook, and, trying these, drifted along the edge of weed rafts. I tempted some trout to take them when there was no fly coming down. This led me to believe that when there was no floating fly coming down the trout were still cruising along the weeds on the look-out for emerging nymphs which might have been of many species. But on those days I had not hit on the value of the marrow scoop and had no means of finding out, though in *Minor Tactics of the Chalk Stream* I wrote of the imitation of nymphs.

Harris

NOT LONG after the conclusion of the 1914–18 disturbance the little Abbotts Barton Syndicate acquired a new member, a member of the Flyfishers' Club named Harris. Though some inches over 6 ft. in height, he had come through the battles of that war without a scratch and looked in beautiful health. It fell to me to introduce him to the water. He had previously had a rod on the Ramsbury length of the Kennet.

Our first day together was a bright spring day. We entered the meadows by the gate opposite Durngate Mill. We were early. Nothing was doing until we reached the meadow opposite the patch backing on to Winnal St. Magdalen Church, when we saw a fine hatch of a biggish light-coloured spring dun proceeding and a large trout backing rather rapidly downstream in the centre taking fly after fly greedily. I had on a rather large hackled fly, the dressing of which I somehow foolishly omitted to record. The hackle was a bright pale blue, the body of a white wool dubbing with an admixture of seal's, the proportions and colours of which I forget. Harris opened fire on a trout, shortening his line as the fish dropped back a foot or two after inspecting and refusing the fly at each cast. I was close behind Harris, and after the third or fourth refusal he said, "You have a go." I dropped my fly almost alongside the trout, which promptly edged over and took it and was hooked. It made a violent rush for the corner where the stream turns down towards the mill and came unstuck.

I gave Harris a fly of the same pattern and left him the stretch from McCaskie's Corner down. I began above the bend at the corner and in a few minutes brought in a handsome fish of exactly 3 lb.

Harris was quite a good fisherman and did as well as any other member of the syndicate, but that was not good enough for him. He wanted the four-brace days which he had been accustomed to get on the Kennet at Ramsbury, and resigned from the Itchen Syndicate at the end of his first session. But the four-brace days were not to be his. Before the next season began the minute flu-germ did for poor Harris what the German rifle-fire and artillery had failed to do and, despite his magnificent physique, put him underground.

Pathetic

———◄◦►———

ONE FINE summer Saturday morning during the 1914–18 War I was down early by Itchen and had arrived at the first stretch above the city where the river runs for a short stretch west to east, when I became aware of a small khaki-clad figure standing on the opposite bank and handling a bottom-fishing rod and line quite skilfully, and apparently wholly unconscious that he was a trespasser and a would-be poacher at that. Had he not been in uniform I should without hesitation have ordered him off, but the poor little Yorkshire lad was so keen and was handling his gear so hopefully and skilfully that, reflecting on the fate he might soon have to face across the Channel and that he might never again have a chance of enjoying sport with rod and line, I could not bring myself to do my duty to the other members of my syndicate by interfering. I knew he had little or no chance of a trout, and that grayling were extremely rare in that part of the water, and I was even tempted to see if I could not catch a trout and offer to hook it on to his line, so that he might not go in fishless. Alas, it was a bad day, and over two hours had elapsed before I caught one to offer him, and when I got back to the place where he had been fishing the pathetic little figure had vanished and I saw him no more. I could only hope that he had betaken himself to the city waters, where float and bait fishing is permitted—and that his efforts were not in vain.

A New Rod

———◀◦▶———

I WAS trying out a new Leonard rod (recently presented to me by a grateful client), 9 ft. 6 in. of exquisite split cane in three joints which was destined later to become the special adoration of my good friend, Dr. E.A. Barton, and to be dubbed by him "Matilda".

The part of the Abbotts Barton stretch of the main Itchen, which the south-east direction of the wind bade me select for the test, was that immediately above and more or less sheltered by the little wood, a spinney, above the gasworks and between the railway lines and the river. One could not, therefore, cast from the left bank till one stood a few yards upstream of the spinney, and as, even there, behind one's hand there was a thick and high growth of feathery reeds, casting could only be done by a combination of switch and roll cast. The time of year was just after the July weed cutting, and sizeable rafts of cut weed lay moored at intervals along the right bank of the river.

There was no obvious hatch of fly coming down, but presently in each of two little bays under the right bank a short way upstream of my stance I saw a swirl, indicating the absorption of a nymph by a sizeable trout. My casting line, a new Carbis No. 3, double tapered, had been duly greased, and the 3-yd. gut cast tapered to 4X with an additional point of 4X gut had been lightly oiled down to the 4X, and for nymph I had selected a pattern which had served me well on the previous day.

Hook	No. 14 down-eyed Pennell hook
Body	Pale greenish floss silk
Whisks	Pale olive cock guinea fowl's neck 3 strands
Thorax	Hare's ear
Legs	Honey dun hen's hackle—short.

It took several lengthening casts, each delivered with care to avoid being hung up on the reeds behind the hand, to get the nymph close up to and near the top of the weed raft, in the lower of the two bays, before the floating gut drew sharply under and my immediate response showed me that I was into something solid. The need not to scare the upper riser bade me turn the hooked trout down, but I could not take him far because of the trees of the spinney overhanging the river. All went well, however, and I was presently able to get my landing net under and to dish out a trout of 2 lb. 13 oz. The contents of his stomach extracted by a marrow spoon and washed into an enamelled metal mug proved the correctness of my selection of nymph, so I lost no time in presenting it to the upper riser; again I saw the floating end of my cast drawn smartly under, and again my immediate response resulted in the sound hooking of a real fish. So strong was he that, as he dashed downstream under the west bank, he stripped off nearly the whole of the casting line from the reel before I could turn him. On account of the overhanging branches of the spinney I dared not follow him downstream, and my only hope was to turn him before it was too late and to draw him firmly but gently upstream till I had him high enough above the spinney to play him with some confidence.

So putting on all the side strain I dared, with nearly the whole of the line beyond the rod tip under water, I got his head round and he came across under my bank. I dared not wind in line at this stage lest the chip of the reel should scare him, so started to pull in line by hand, and presently I led him across a bit of sandy bottom— which enabled me to get some idea of his dimensions. I had No. 1 to give me an indication, and that left me in no doubt that he topped 4 lb. by a good margin. He was, of course, far from beaten, but he was suffering himself to be led so quietly that I was able to get him ten or twelve yards above the spinney before I realised the presence just in front of him of a formidable snag. I had therefore to turn him down, and he came along quietly close to my bank when I foolishly put the net into the water in his path. Catching sight of it or me awoke him to consciousness of his danger and in a flash he was out in mid-stream and smashed my 4X point like park thread. There was nothing doing upstream to the big railway arch, and, too disheartened to continue fishing, I went in with my single capture.

The Red Hole

A FEW hundred yards above the Durngate Mill and at no great distance below the city bathing place in the north-east corner of the park, the western stream of the Abbotts Barton water divides into two streams, about half the current passing through two brick arches into a round deepish pool a nice cast across, then turning and running under a bridge of planking—to follow parallel the part that bounds the park and to be known as Swift Lake. Swift Lake seldom contains a sizeable trout, yet Red Hole, as the round pool below the brick arches is known, has yielded me and my friends and guests many a sturdy trout, rarely scaling less than 2 lb.

It was from the upper brick arch that "Wary Willie", whose passing was described in *Minor Tactics of the Chalk Stream*, was extracted, but he was caught from the park side (the west) of the side stream before the park ground was acquired by Winchester and made into a park. The pool known as the Red Hole seldom showed a trout much further than a couple of yards below the two brick arches and Swift Lake seldom showed a trout at all—yet the Red Hole was always worth a few casts close up to one or other of the brick arches, preferably the northern one.

At one time, and one only, do I recall a good trout lying for two successive week-ends in Swift Lake, a yard or two below the planking bridge, and, not realising that he was there or even suspecting that a sizeable fish might be there, I put him down. At the follow-ing week-end I had as my guest an officer who had the V.C. after his name, for some feat of gallantry on the Afghan frontiers, and I had provided him with a 10 ft. 6¾ oz. Leonard rod, carrying a No. 3 line dressed by N.D. Coggeshall. We crossed the lower side stream from the park by a boat from the south-east corner, and walked up between the stream we had crossed and Swift Lake till near the planking, when I told my guest of the trout I had seen and recommended him to wait and, if the fish were there and rose, to offer him the home-made red sedge which I provided. The fish was there and took the fly at the first offer—but was missed in the strike. He was, however, so little alarmed that before many minutes he rose again. My guest was about to cast, but I recommended a change of fly as the fish had had reason to suspect the red sedge as a "wrong un" and he was in a place where there was no regular hatch, and I tied on a Tup's Indispensable. A few minutes later I had the satisfaction of netting out for my guest a nice stout fish of 2 lb. 3 oz.

Another guest of mine whom I led to the Red Hole was the famous Dr. Francis Ward. Him also I provided with a little red sedge—and I saved him from a smash, possibly involving rod top, at the planking bridge, by telling him how to turn his fish and keep it in the pool when it was mad to get away under the plank bridge. That was another two-pounder. Dr. Francis Ward came again on several occasions and seldom failed to visit the Red Hole and get a two-pounder.

Whether I entered the meadows at Durngate Mill or at the park corner, by boat I seldom omitted to cast a red sedge at the brick arches, and I cannot say how many two-pounders were extracted by my friends—Dr. Norman McCaskie of Green Cat fame and others—from that marvellous Red Hole.

THE SMALL HUT

One never saw the trout lying below the brick arches—but if one kept on casting for a while there was often a response sooner or later. I remember one evening when Dr. McCaskie and I came up together along Swift Lake and he gave up after casting fifteen or twenty minutes at the Red Hole. Within five minutes of his leaving disappointed for the main river I was busy playing a 2 lb. 6 oz. trout.

I remember leaving a riser just above the cottage by Winnal St. Magdalen to rest him, going to the Red Hole and getting a two-pounder and offering the same red sedge on my return to the trout I had rested, and taking it with a dash. I made no secret of the spot—but none of the other members of the syndicate ever made much of it.

I suspect the reason was little red sedge.

Picking It Off

I N, I think, the second of my immortal works (from the first of which my good friend Fleur de Lys kindly suggested the dropping of the t), I described a casting manoeuvre designed to relieve a delicate rod of strain while getting the line off the water and into the air with the minimum of drying effect on the cast and fly or nymph. I called it "picking it off"; and other anglers fishing the same water some distance away would vow that they could identify me by the action of my rod when "picking it off"—though at far too great a distance from me to distinguish me by clothing or feature.

In "picking it off", after a cast had been delivered and had been carried down by the current past its objective, by a side-way swing of the rod top one heaved almost all of the casting line in a sort of wide loop into the air while the gut and a yard or so of the casting line remained in the water. The next move of the rod brought the rest of the casting line and the gut and fly or nymph, still wet, into the air when the cast was completed in the way usual with a dry fly, only neither gut nor fly nor nymph was dry. For nymph or wet-fly fishing under a far bank "picking it off" was ideal, and I have heard skilled anglers call it a highly coloured miracle, though these were not the qualifying words that were used.

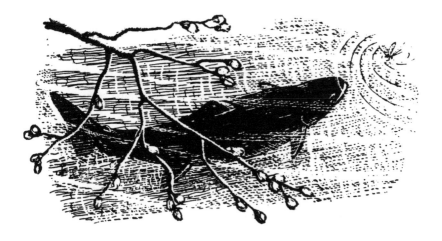

I should have difficulty in saying what, in terms of trout, that manœuvre has been worth to me—or in picking one incident rather than another in illustration—but I can say this, that it enables one to present fly or nymph to a trout or more than one more speedily and accurately than any other manœuvre I know.

I recall an occasion in August 1911 when, in a pocket under the eastern bank of the main stream, I descried no less than five trout busily feeding under water. The pocket was bounded by big hairy tussocks about a yard apart in which it would be fatal to be hung up, yet, by the manœuvre of "picking it off" I was able on that bright sunny afternoon to hook on my Tup's Indispensable and to bring out, without scaring any of them, all five of these busy trout.

On a later occasion a purist (who strongly disliked my wet-fly and nymph methods) was at Rolt's Stile and pointed to a break in the opposite bank through which the river, being full, was pouring into the meadow beyond. In the gap lay a tidy trout obviously feeding, and he challenged me to get that fish. It was July and I had on the nymph of the July dun. The very first cast with the "picking it off" manœuvre, which reached and entered the gap, was marked by the sudden side-way turn of the trout and by his being led next moment into the river and across to the landing net and being put at the disposal of the purist. A similar incident led to the enthusiastic conversion of a guest who had wished to know how it was done, and by the end of the day he had been able to secure a brace.

Mullins

◄O►

IN THE latter years of my fifty-six years' spell of fishing the Itchen the head-keeper of the Abbotts Barton stretch rented by our little syndicate was a middle-aged but very robust Irishman named Mullins. He seemed to be a mascot to me, but to poachers he was a lesson.

One early morning he was (he told me) concealed in an irrigation ditch watching a small group of sunfrocked poachers in an upper meadow. They were right upon him without having detected his presence, and one of them, who had concealed not only the baldness of his pate but a complete clutch of partridge eggs, as Mullins well knew, said to the others, "I wish I knew where that b—— Mullins was." Next moment a huge hand descended startlingly on the speaker's hat, smashing every egg and sending the yolk streaming over face and neck. Our Irish keeper proclaimed, "Now you know where that b—— Mullins is."

Restrictions

———◀o▶———

AS TIME went by after the 1914–18 War was over, particularly after the admission to the syndicate of a certain wealthy member, restrictions on the number of days on which members might have a guest grew ever tighter and tighter and ultimately the only way in which a member might give a friend a day was by sharing a rod with him. At the time I thought the restriction a grievance and both illiberal and unnecessary. Looking back on its results, I can see that it had the merit of bringing me to closer and often very pleasant relations with men whom otherwise I would probably never have got to know so well, and it gave me opportunities of exchanging views and demonstrating methods which I should otherwise not have had.

For instance, there was the late Sir John Francis. He came down one July week-end to share my rod, and as we approached the main stream by the path crossing the middle of the meadows he asked me to demonstrate my method of using an artificial nymph. We reached the main just downstream of the ditch which divides the meadow from the tussocky patch by the gasworks, and, as luck would have it, just at the moment when a nice sizeable trout put out from a tiny bay in the east bank to take something invisible and return to his hide. I tied on a dark mole's-fur-bodied nymph much like a favourite pattern of John Younger, wetted it with saliva and dropped it in the mouth of the bay, and next minute was leading the trout out of his hiding-hole to cross the river and eventually to my net. Sir John was highly intrigued and delighted and, taking my rod, was not long in achieving a brace of nice trout in similar conditions.

Another and a much older friend was the late Dr. Norman McCaskie of Green Cat fame. He was a good dry-fly rod and a successful Tweed angler and had been my guest on numerous occasions before the restrictions rule came into force which only allowed a guest to share a member's rod. As a result, he had never taken to the artificial nymph till his last day on the Itchen with me. It was a July day and the trout were obviously nymphing, and, having once experienced the pleasure of hooking good fish on the *right* nymph, Dr. McCaskie took up the game with enthusiasm and took in our three-brace limit—all good fish.

Others who shared my rod on occasion were: an Indian Lord Chief Justice (retired), his son (then a major), Dr. Francis Ward of *Animal Life under Water*, and others.

Bulls

————◀O▶————

IN OCTOBER 1892 the influenza epidemic which claimed so many victims sent me down with double pneumonia, and it took a two-month sea trip to the Cape and Durban and back to London in the same vessel and then a couple of years of quiet and care to put me together again—and then I had not fully regained my strength. But in 1895 I was kneeling by the Itchen some 150 yds. above McCaskie's Corner, when, hearing a snort behind me, I turned and became aware of a huge brown bull charging the fence just below the corner. When I saw him clear it like a deer and realised that there was only one fence, and that a smaller one, between Taurus and me, I quickly decided that I had business elsewhere, so, collecting my bags and landing net, I made off under forced draught towards a small footbridge which crosses the western branch of the Itchen alongside of a trunk which on occasion carried water from the main or eastern channel across the western to irrigate the meadows. I listened for a moment to see what the bull would do about the smaller fence, and, seeing him sail over it like a bird, I decided that my retreat must continue, and I reached the footbridge in time to get on to it while the bull was racing up the west bank of the ben 30 or 40 yds. behind. Then, to my astonishment, he plunged into the main river and, swimming across, climbed out on the east side.

In those days, the meadows on the east side had not been abandoned to flooding as they were later and were, for pasture, producing a rent of £6 or £7 an acre, and they were divided into two by a stout fence too high for the bull to jump. I then realised that the herd of cows on the north side of the fence, and not I, had been the animal's objective, for he raced up and down one side of the fence while the cows with kinks in their tails and in a violent state of excitement romped up and down the other. Eventually men armed with pitchforks and staves drove a very resentful bull back to the exit from the bottom of the lower meadow to his proper home.

On another occasion I was coming in at dusk from an evening on the side stream and had one meadow to pass, when I became aware that on the far side of a shallow irrigation ditch 8 or 10 ft. wide and nearly empty a bull was keeping pace with me. I dared not put on speed, being certain that if I did the bull would give chase. So I walked quietly along my side of the stretch to the gate which was the exit and was thankful to get through uninjured.

But my troubles were not over yet. My lovely little 9 ft. 5 oz. Leonard rod had not been taken down, and, having got into the lane which led to the farm buildings, I found myself almost among a herd of horses in a violent state of excitement and I had to jam myself against the fence and hold my priceless rod out of danger to let them charge past.

On yet another occasion I was making for the Rolt's Stile at the top of the meadow in which the hut Piscatoribus Sacrum then stood. As I neared the stile I became aware that the animal which stood, almost nosing it, was not, as I supposed, a cow but a bull. It was too late to retreat. I could only go forward and I surmounted the stile unmolested. But no sooner had I passed than the bull turned, rushed violently at a haystack recently erected in his meadow and, butting it savagely, tore out chunks of hay with his horns. On my last visit, this time as a guest of the landlord, during the last war, I found the meadows occupied by no fewer than six herds, each complete with bull.

One of the Sons

——◄o►——

IT WAS my good fortune to count among my professional and angling friends a barrister (subsequently a judge), referred to in some of my papers as Fleur de Lys, and to him I owe my introduction to one of the sons of the learned man who wrote that charming book, *Letters to a Salmon Fisher's Sons*. To Fleur de Lys do I also owe the suggestion that I should invite that son to fish the Abbotts Barton length of the Itchen with me. I took Fleur de Lys' advice and I found that in the person of the son there was not only a first-rate performer with the wet fly on rough streams but one who had the gumption to bring his knowledge of the wet fly on rough streams to bear on the problems of chalkstream angling, including in particular the case of the artificial nymph. In this respect he proved the most satisfying performer of all whom from first to last I had to fish with me that difficult, but, for that very difficulty, that most enchanting water. He proved to be not only an outstanding angler but a highly skilled and intelligent fly (and nymph) observer, with whom it was a real pleasure to work as well as to fish.

I recall that there was 100 yds. or thereabouts of fine holding water, from which, fishing from the right bank, I have had seven trout, but seldom could lure, casting from the left bank, a single fish lying under the right—and they nearly all lay under the right bank—but the son seemed to find no difficulty in getting them to his fly or nymph.

End of a Problem

ON THE east bank of the western stream, opposite the Ducks'
Nest Spinney, the river is fringed with a row of large
tussocks, under which a string of trout might almost invariably be
found. Yet for many years they proved to be for me, and not for
me only, an almost insoluble problem, for it was a rare thing for
one of them to be caught—at any rate until I found a method of
approaching them from the west bank. For long this seemed
impossible; the trees of the spinney closely lined the west bank, so
that to attempt to stretch a line behind one was to ask for a disastrous hang-up.

But early in the century a Bavarian experience put me in the way
of solving the problem. During a May holiday spent on that fascinating river, the Erlaubnitz, my small party lodged for quite half of
our three weeks' stay in a riverside hostelry, Zum Weison Ross,
taking our meals at tables under lime trees growing close to the
river's edge. On the far side of the stream was a thick thorn hedge
bounding a main road. And as we sat at breakfast (with our lines
trailing in the river to soak the gut) we could not fail to observe the
rising of trout which at that hour had already started feeding boldly
under the thorn hedge. Breakfast disposed of, I could not, while
waiting for the rest of my party, resist the temptation to try to put
my alder to the trout under the hedge. It was my first experience of

switching—and naturally I had some hang-ups—but so rapidly did I improve that by the time we left there was scarce a trout under the hedge opposite the inn grounds.

When I got back to the Itchen, therefore, I was equipped with enough experience to lead me to assail the trout under the tussocks from between the trees which pretty closely lined the river bank for the whole length of the spinney. I found my lovely little 5-oz. 9-ft. Leonard the ideal weapon for the game, provided that the wind was not strongly from the east, and the trout, which, fished from the east bank over the tussocks, had been so scary, proved quite simple-minded when covered with a switch from between the trees lining the spinney bank.

I remember J.R., one of our members, jeering at me for attempting a trout at the upstream end of the row of tussocks, and being quite astonished when he saw the arch of my little stick as the hook bit home.

From that time on the fish under the tussocks ceased to be a problem. As I stood in the spinney the stream came from left to right. Pulling line off the reel, I let the current take it until I estimated that it was nearly enough to reach the far bank; then, raising the rod top so as to lift most of the line off the water, I would make a downward and forward cut which would belly the line and bring the gut and fly off the water and extend the line straight across river before me. If it was not out enough to reach the lie of the fish, a little more line was easily let out and the cast repeated till the right length was attained. If I saw no fly going down I often used a small pheasant tail with good effect. Tup's Indispensable was another pretty sure solution—two brace was a not uncommon bag from the 50 yds. or so of tussock bank if the wind were not adverse and strong.

McCaskie's Last Day

————◄o►————

O N 26th June 1938 (in my eightieth year and very last on my dearly loved Itchen) my good friend, Dr. Norman McCaskie— yes, McCaskie of the Green Cat—was to have his birthday on that length which I had been fishing every season since May 1883.

For a string of years previous to 1938 conditions on that water had not been entirely happy. It was not only that my experimental and pioneer work in establishing the use of the artificial nymph as a fair and legitimate method of taking chalk-stream trout was not approved by all the other members of the little syndicate which rented the Abbotts Barton fishery, but several years earlier a new member had been elected whose activities from the first had not been conducive to the maintenance of the happy spirit which had hitherto prevailed among the members; and though he had resigned his membership several years previously (dying shortly after), that happy spirit had never been entirely recovered and the uncomfort- able spirit which has been brought into the whole functions and proceedings of the syndicate persisted among the members years after that member had resigned and died.

Although his introduction to the water should have satisfied him that that water was well stocked, yet he never missed an opportu- nity of proposing some fresh restriction upon the privileges of members, and for some reason which I never succeeded in comprehending he invariably succeeded in persuading the other members that the restriction he was for the moment proposing was demanded by the circumstances of the water; and as invariably I found myself in a minority of one, he also led the other members into voting for expenditure on restocking, the only effect of which was to send down into the city waters shoals of little fish to be caught in scores by the city anglers in the Weirs with maggots and worms. The number of days on which a member might have a guest on the water was more and more narrowly restricted, until in the previous year, though the number of members of the syndicate had declined from six to four, the only terms on which a member might have a guest to fish with him were that he must either share his rod with his guest or let the guest do all the fishing. In either case the number of fish that might be taken was one member's quota. More and more I resented these restrictions, and I would have resigned in 1937 if I could have found another water approximately as good and as accessible, but I had not done so, and had paid my subscription for the season of 1938 in June, and only in the ensuing April did I find myself able to secure for that and the two following years a rod on the Nadder with the privilege of having a friend to fish with me.

Thus it came about that on the last occasion when I would have the pleasure and privilege of entertaining my friend McCaskie on the Itchen we were confined to one rod between us. That rod, however, was that little 9-ft. miracle of split cane from the U.S.A. which had been the joy of my life since it was given to me by a life-long friend in 1905.

As July was at hand, I had tied an ample stock of nymph of the July dun, and I may say at once that it proved an entirely correct solution. Having come down to Winchester overnight, and having no need to spend any part of the morning on fly dressing, I was able to make an early start.

THE RAILWAY BRIDGE

It was a lovely morning, more like July than June, and it was not long after ten o'clock when the Nuns' Walk, alongside the little Hyde Brook, took us to the keeper's hut on the side stream. I took McCaskie there, because on two or three previous occasions I had spotted a handsome two-pounder under the west bank of the side stream just above the weed rack and, having on each occasion risen him without succeeding in hooking him, I wished to give my friend the chance of seeing whether he could do any better. His luck, however, was out, for though, like me, he rose the fish, he failed to hook him, and he handed back my little Leonard to me. A cast upstream under the east bank brought me a trout of 1½ lb. and then we made our way across the meadows eastward to the main stream, reaching it just above the clump of tall trees on the far side of the river. Thence we crept slowly up to the railway arch (which was now the top limit of the water) without finding a feeding trout, thence slowly down again to the clump, still finding nothing doing; then McCaskie insisted on my taking the rod, and just above the clump I caught another one-and-a-half-pounder but returned it in the hope of better fish.

McCaskie found nothing doing opposite the clump and handed back the rod. Nothing was rising under the east bank alongside of the tussock paddock on the downstream side of the clump, but the bright sun enabled me to spot a good fish lying deep on the clay-coloured bottom and, when I saw him move out just as my nymph was approaching, and then turn back to resume his position under the bank, I tightened and, as I fully expected, hooked the trout, and presently McCaskie netted him out for me—2½ lb. The rest of the water under the tussock bank was undisturbed—and McCaskie had not fished many yards down it before he had hooked another fish which put up a prolonged fight but came unstuck at the net. Bad luck. I will not recount our further experiences of that day in detail. But for the first time McCaskie got the knack of rising and hooking the trout on a nymph, and though several of his fish had to go back we took in two and a half brace—best fish 2½ lb. His getting the knack was a great pleasure to me, and my only regret was that we were to have no more of the Itchen together.

Great Men and Trout

———◄o►———

URING THE many seasons from May 1883 to the end of
August 1938 that I was privileged to fish the Abbotts Barton
stretch of the Itchen extending from Kingsworthy to Winchester I
met on the riverside a number of outstanding anglers, from Francis
Francis and William Senior at the one end of the scale to Major
John Waller Hills and Colonel E.W. Harding near the other end,
and during that stretch of time my catch of three-pounder trout
only totalled a dozen. Major Hills is remembered for a number of
books, of which *A Summer on the Test* and his *History of Flyfishing*
are perhaps the best known. Colonel Harding, on the other hand,
died not long after his first and only book, *The Fly Fisher and the
Trout's Point of View*, was published, but that volume earned him
the tribute from a distinguished American angler (Mr. Eugene V.
Connell III) of being one of the two greatest angling minds of
Britain. The purpose of this "Memory" is to connect each of these
with an occasion of the capture of one of these twelve three-
pounders when he was a guest of mine on the Itchen.

My acquaintance with Colonel Harding did not last long. It
began when he was at work on his great book, but during the
course of it he came down to Winchester to fish the Itchen with me
and to talk over and work out his problems on a number of occasions. I cannot name the precise date or even the year of which I am

writing, but it must have been in the late twenties or in 1930. I had
left him busy with a good trout which was rising or rather taking
nymphs close to the left bank just above the spot where the town
lads came down to bathe in the short straight bit of the main stream
which runs towards the church of Winnal St. Magdalen, and I had
recommended him, when he had to look for another good trout, to
seek it at the well-known spot close to the swans' nest opposite
McCaskie's Corner while I moved slowly up the right bank along
the straight coming down to McCaskie's Corner in search of a
feeding trout. Colonel Harding had got his two-pounder and was
fishing towards the swans' nest before I found a riser. Then I spotted a tiny dimple another 200 yds. up the straight, and, keeping
low, I ran to take position opposite. At the end of my cast tapered
to 4X was a tiny nymph, dressed on a short square-bend sneck
hook of Bartlett's B7362 pattern (now no longer obtainable and
even then dating back to before 1914), which C.A. Hassam

affected. The trout had not risen again, and, after watching some minutes, I cast to the spot where I expected him to be, and next moment some intuition bade me raise my rod tip. It bowed gracefully to the fish that had sucked in the tiny peril and a ding-dong battle ensued, and went on, till the fish had reached the spot where Colonel Harding knelt just above McCaskie's Corner. I apologised for having had to yield to *force majeure*, but by then my trout was fairly beaten and the Colonel whipped him out with his landing net. My spring balance said exactly 3 lb. and I had to cut the tiny hook (smaller than the 000 of other makes) from the hard tough gristly tip of my trout's snout. I put down his long and stubborn resistance to the fact that he was hooked in the most insensitive part of his entire anatomy.

The incident which occurred when Major Waller Hills was the guest occurred a few years later, after a weed-rack with a plank bridge across the side stream had been constructed at the top of the straight above Ducks' Nest Spinney and another on the main a few yards above the boathouse.

Major Hills had come down with me for his first week-end on a Friday afternoon, and we entered the meadows from the Nuns' Walk and came together up the side stream to casting distance below the weed rack where I knew there were several good trout close together. The Major had a rod which, he told me, Mr. Lunn had said was the best split cane owned by any member of the Houghton Club. I did not greatly like it; it struck me as harsh in action, but I recommended him to try the fish below the weed rack with a red sedge I gave him, and after he had fished out the spot to cross the weed rack to the inner meadow and to make for the boathouse on the main and to fish the length below it and above, using orange quill as soon as the rise forms, indicating B.W.O., occurred. Meanwhile I pursued the side stream to Five Hatches, incidentally catching on Tup's Indispensable and returning three trout under our 1½-lb. limit, thence made my way to Rolt's Stile, so-called because H.A. Rolt, K.C., when a member, lodging for his weekly visits in Kingsworthy, used to turn back on reaching that stile. I found nothing doing on the generally well-stocked stretch below the stile and leant on it for a few moments to watch the length above. Presently I saw the Major making his way across Winnal Moor towards the boathouse on the main, and then, hearing the sound of a suck, I turned and saw a ring a couple of dozen yards upstream under the far bank—the east. (I have not mentioned that my cast was a new Reinforce tapered to its nominal 4X, slightly stouter than Hercules 4X but finer than Hercules 3X.) I got over the stile and knelt to cast to the spot where the fish had risen; but as I did so, knowing that it was getting late, I looked at my watch, which said four minutes to nine. Then I cast and at once the fish reached out and sucked in the Indispensable. It was evidently a very strong fish, but the cathedral clock chimed nine as I clambered over Rolt's Stile with the trout still upstream of it. The straight stretch below the stile was a very weedy bit of river, and I was glad that my gut was a bit stouter than a normal 4X, for each time that I steered that obstinate trout to my bank it no sooner caught sight of me than it turned and tore through weed bed after weed bed till it brought up again at the far bank, then I would engineer it back through weed bed after weed bed till it was under my bank and then it liked me so little it stripped the line off my reel and through weed bed after weed bed it found a limit in the far bank. Before I had brought the fish the 100 yds. or so to the next bend, the cathedral chimes rang the quarter-past, and 50 yds. or so below the bend they chimed the half-hour, with the trout apparently as tireless as ever. I began to wish that he would come unstuck, having no desire to be fighting him all night.

But at last I saw an off-chance of putting an end to the battle, for a few yards further downstream on my side there was a large raft of cut weed lodged against the bank, and two or three minutes later, as the fish came over to my side I rushed his head into the weed raft. Then, slipping the net in behind him, I dug him out and landed him, still kicking furiously and still full of fight, on my bank.

Then I looked at my watch, which read nine-thirty-six, so that that amazing fish had fought me for forty minutes. I took him along in the net to join the Major. I found that after rising and scratching three trout at the weed raft on the side stream, he had killed a sizeable trout on the main on an orange quill.

My fish was then weighed and scaled 3 lb. easily, to my disappointment. I had expected something nearer 4 lb. Again I had to dig out my hook from the tough, gristly tip of his nose. I had to infer that it was the insensitive character of that part which made him put up such an astonishing fight—almost as though he had been foul-hooked.

Then we reeled up to go in. Doing so, I examined my cast and was amazed to find that it showed scarcely any sign of the ordeal it had survived. My rod was my little 9-ft. 5½-oz. Leonard, presented to me in 1905, and forty years later, when I gave up fishing, as good as ever.

A Great Angling Mind

———◄o►———

A MONG THE distinguished anglers I have met, quite a good few have fished the Abbotts Barton length of the Itchen. There was H.S. Hall (of eyed-hook fame), four angling editors of the *Field*, Francis Francis, William Senior (Red Spinner), C.H. Cook (John Bickerdyke), H.T. Sheringham, F.M. Halford, and among my personal guests I have had Dr. Francis Ward (author of *Animal Life under Water*), C.A.N. Wauton (author of *Ephemeridae*), George M.L. La Branche (author of *The Dry Fly on Fast Water*) and Lamorna Birch, R.A., among others. But of all whom I have met either there or elsewhere none made a greater impression on me— not so much as a catcher of fish but as a great angling mind—than Colonel E. West Harding, who fished there with me during the period of incubation and writing of his outstanding book, *The Fly Fisher and the Trout's Point of View*.

I made the Colonel's acquaintance one evening when I was occu- pying the chair of Mr. Vice at dinner at the Flyfishers' Club, when Major Saffery, the secretary, brought him along and introduced him as a new member who wished to make my acquaintance; and from that moment for the few, the pitifully few years before death claimed him we were friends, meeting not only at his home and at mine but on the Abbotts Barton length of the Itchen while he was working out theories and principles which he disclosed to the world in his great book. After its publication he was at work not only on a new edition but on entirely new and more advanced theories which he did not live to put into shape for publication; nor were his notes in such shape as to enable anyone to translate them into a book. An American correspondent of Harding's, my friend Eugene V. Connell III, did more than any other writer to elucidate Harding's teaching in a part of his beautiful volume, *Random Casts*.

It is a curious fact that as a practical angler Harding was not brilliant. Though I gave him all the opportunities I could on the pretty numerous occasions when he was my guest on the Abbotts Barton length, he was not a highly accurate or delicate caster. Whether that was attributable to the defects of his fly rod or to nervous maladjustment I could never determine. It was a great pity, for theoretically he was, in my judgment, quite the foremost angling mind of the century.

An Early Phase in the Evolution of the Artificial Nymph

———◄○►———

IN MY early Itchen days I was puzzled, after a weed cutting, to note that at times at least one fish would put up close alongside of a weed raft when there was no sign of any floating natural insect being borne down by the current. Sometimes there would be two. These things were specially noticeable when the weed rafts yellowed and stacked. I soon found by trial and error that on these occasions the trout were not often attracted by a split-winged floating artificial dun, but would occasionally take a floating red sedge fairly confidently. Still, the fish were obviously feeding on something below the surface, and as the rises that occurred were seldom twice exactly at the same place it struck me that they might be cruising up and down on the watch for some subaqueous form of life emerging from the weed raft; then I chanced to get a couple of blue macaw feathers, the individual strands of which, wound on a hook, showed a yellow quill with a blue rib, and I tied a few with red macaw tails. I also used similar feathers of other birds for bodies. The hooks were tiny down eye Limericks and these patterns proved rather more effective than the red sedges—and for a while I used them. This was before I discovered the virtues of the marrow scoop in extracting the contents of a trout's stomach. After that I was able to make systematic efforts to represent nymphal forms with due attention

alike to shape, colour and dimensions, and the blue macaws and
other experiments went into discard.

A Singular Sunday

———◄o►———

I WAS down on the river for a solitary week-end, it being one of those week-ends when the laws of the syndicate, which, unlike those of the Medes and Persians, which alter not, kept altering annually for the worse, forbade me to have a guest to fish with me, and I had crossed the side stream by the plank bridge near the hut (Piscatoribus Sacrum), which was later to be burnt down at night by some of those town ruffians who were too superior to believe in private property, when I became aware of four rod-bearing figures coming across the meadows to cross the side stream by the same plank bridge. They were two of the members whose turn it was to have a guest, each member accompanied by his guest. It was the decent convention of the syndicate always to give the guest the choice of water and any other advantages that he might fancy or be advised to take—so I delayed putting up my rod till the party of four had crossed the side stream, and the guests had been introduced and had put up their rods.

While they and their hosts were preparing I kept my eye on the east bank to which what little wind there was was drifting, and I spotted a tiny dimple which broke the surface directly opposite and called attention to it; but it was not inspected and none of the four seemed impressed, and presently, their preparations completed, they drifted upstream and I completed mine before they had gone very far, by mounting a tiny nymph. Still the dimple did not recur—but I had noted fairly precisely the tussock in the east bank under which I had seen it, and I made a single cast to a point a foot or so upstream, and next moment, responding to an infinitesimal signal, I raised my rod tip and fastened in the trout. He was not 2 lb. but was quite a sizeable fish. But—I did not get another all day. Nor did either of the two other members or their guests. There was no hatch of fly. It was the only trout taken that day.

Introduction and Exit

———◀◉▶———

I DO not recall the man's name, nor who proposed him for membership of the Abbotts Barton Syndicate. The date of his joining must have been after 1905, the year which brought me my lovely little 9-ft. Leonard; but, whenever it was, his proposer asked me to show him over the water and to put him in the way of things. We met for a Saturday evening, and as I had collected my three brace during the afternoon I left my rod at the keeper's and took the new member on to the east bank, crossing the derelict field which adjoins the little church of Winnal St. Magdalen. The new member had quite a new 10-ft. Leonard split cane, a replica of my

pair which the 9-ft. little beauty had relegated to retirement, and he put it together, ran his line through the bridge rings and rove on his 3 yds. of tapered cast.

A quarter of an hour's wait showed nothing doing in the short 100 yds. below McCaskie's Corner, but just round the point a trout put up close to our bank. There was nothing to show what the fish was taking and, on chance, I rove on one of my little red sedges. The new member cast quite a nice straight line and crossed the place of the rise accurately, and at the third or fourth offer up came the trout. N.M. (for new member) struck and missed, putting the trout down.

Will it be believed that the incident was repeated no less than nine times in the 300 yds. which brought us to the corner opposite the long spinney which ended on the west bank of the side stream? Just round that corner, however, it could be seen that there was a light show of pale spinners in the air, and, taking the hint, I replaced the red sedge with a pale Tup's Indispensable on a 00 Pennell Sneck. N.M.'s luck persisted—but with a difference. By the time we had reached the bend opposite the boathouse N. M. had hooked nine trout, come unstuck seven times and been broken twice.

In the meantime the evening had moved on and the shape of the rings under our bank gave evidence that the trout were liking B.W.O. So I supplied him with an orange quill on a No. I Hall's Snecky Limerick. By the time we had reached the point opposite Rolt's Stile the rise was over. N.M. had fished to four more trout, had risen all of them, missed one, hooked but lost two, and at the last moment had saved an entire blank by killing a trout of 1 lb. 9 oz.

Soon it had grown dark and the keeper was waiting to ferry us over the Winnal Moor and land us for the walk back to his cottage.

Though I do not think N.M.'s membership lasted into a third

season, his luck was not always so appallingly bad as on that first evening.

For instance, on one occasion I had spotted a really good trout under the east bank about 100 yds. below the hut Piscatoribus Sacrum, and I was beginning to offer him an iron blue with a cock jackdaw throat hackle—and had good hope of taking him when N.M. came along and squatted down on the bank at my right hand, effectively barring my casting with any degree of accuracy, and began to tell me one of his interminable stories.

In the hope of getting him to move on, I gave him one of my cock jackdaw's iron blues; and then, finding that ineffective and that another romance was on the way, I said I thought I would give that trout a rest and went across to the side stream. When I returned I found N.M. very pleased with N.M. for having caught my trout—approaching 3 lbs.

Then under the willow which marks the end of the muddy stretch running from the railway line at the gasworks to the main river there were, that season, a brace of two-pounders in a spot which in previous seasons had only held one fish. All the members knew these fish and tried them in vain; then one day N.M. caught them both. With some manœuvring I got him to show me the pattern of fly which had done the trick. It was the grossest carica-ture of Greenwell's Glory that I ever saw, roughly tied with gross feathers on a No. 2 hook.

Perils of the Water Meadow

———◄o►———

JUST OPPOSITE the little tussock-ridden square plot on the left bank, which lies between the ditch which cuts it off from that bank and the clump of trees, a ditch about the width of a horse's back divides one meadow from the rest. The grasses growing on each side and overhanging it make it look even smaller and less noticeable. Yet one summer night in B.W.O. time that little ditch was the scene of a tragedy. That night I was on the little tussocky square and had collected a nice brace and had hopes of another, when I became aware from the frightened squealing of a pair of horses—which the growing dark prevented me from seeing—that they were in trouble. I did not know the farmer who rented those meadows or where he dwelt; but, hearing a labourer making for Winchester on the railway line behind me, I asked him if he knew the farmer and where he lived, and on his promise to go to the farmer and tell him that two of his horses were in some trouble and needed help, I felt that I had done all I could and went on fishing. I do not recall with what result.

Next morning, however, I learned that the farmer had not been warned, but there on the bank of the ditch lay an old horse dead and the younger one of the pair had been rescued when up to its jaws in the mud of that terrible little ditch.

Years later a son of the owner of those water meadows told me that the black ditch which joins the side stream at the top of the meadow had been cleaned out, and had contained the skeletons of several cows and horses, thus accounting for a number of missing animals which had been supposed to have been stolen.

The mud in the spinney was so deep that a 10-ft. pole would not reach the bottom.

Colonel Jesse

———◄o►———

ANY YEARS ago, near the end of the nineteenth century, an
early summer morning found me (on my way to Kingsbridge
to unravel a legal tangle) leaving the main-line train at Brent to enter
the local train which was to take me to my destination, and for much
of the way closely followed the lovely little Devonshire Avon—and
I recalled with what delight I looked down upon it as it tumbled
from one deep, clear rocky pool to another—speculating on the type
of fly which I would dress to flick into them.

Except on my return journey a few days after I was never to see
that little Avon again—but it was to be recalled to my memory years
later when, seated at the trout fly-dressing table at the Flyfishers'
Club Piccadilly premises. I made the acquaintance of Colonel Jesse,
then a new member, and found that he frequently fished that enchanting little river. My memories of it moved me to dress for the Colonel
some patterns of the type of trout fly, nearly always on a No. 2 down-
eye Carlisle bend hook. His successes with my patterns moved me to
do so again and again and we became friends.

But by that time the practice of permitting members to have
guests to fish, becoming continually more restricted, had reached
the stage when it could only be effected on terms of the member
sharing his rod with the guest. However, Colonel Jesse seemed so
pleased at the idea of casting a fly on the classic Itchen that it was

at least an equal pleasure to give him his chance.

It was a lovely summer morning when he came, and we started together up the right bank of the main river; but, to our disappointment, till about noon there was no sign of fly on the water and not a rise to be seen. By that time we had arrived at the top of the meadow opposite the little wood by the gasworks. Near our bank was a fly-board two or three yards out in the stream and we were delighted to see a trout putting up several times a minute alongside the fly-board. After watching for a minute, I tied a gold-ribbed hare's ear on an 0 hook and handed my rod (the 9½-ft. Leonard so beloved of Dr. Barton), to the Colonel, and in a few minutes battle was joined. The trout was carefully steered clear of entanglement with the fly-board and presently the net recovered his 2¾ lb.

We worked up to the big railway bridge without seeing another rise and, much disappointed, turned downstream again.

We had got to the bend below the boathouse where the river steers westwards again when I had an idea. I knew a spot at the bend where quite a nice fish had his reputed quarters; and as he was not rising I hoped he might be tempted by a nymph. So, removing the gold-ribbed hare's ear, I tied on a likely nymph and pointed out to the Colonel the exact crinkle of the surface which indicated the spot where I expected the trout to be lying. Cast after fruitless cast he made, and I said, "You have not quite covered the spot yet—give me the rod and I'll show you." My first shot was no better and I made a second.

"Here, take the rod," said I, handing it back to him as it bent to the plunge of the trout. At the bottom of the stretch I had the satisfaction of netting out a sturdy trout of 2 lb. 11 oz. The only fly in the ointment being that missing ounce which was required to make the brace the Colonel took home an even 5½ lbs. We saw no further rise all day.

Eddie Mills, Priddis and My Leonards

———————◄o►———————

I N THE year 1904 at the Crystal Palace there took place a fly-cast-ing tournament, the only one in which I ever took part as a contestant.

The year 1902 brought me the acquaintance (developing into friendship through the light-rod controversy) of the American angler, Nathan Durfie Coggeshall, who invited me to see his Leonard rods. One of these was a ten-footer of soft old-fashioned type, quite unsuited to fishing the dry fly, but the other presented to him by the makers was a 10-ft. Tournament rod in three joints weighing 6½ oz. and was probably the first to come over here to challenge the Houghtons, the Test rod and other dry-fly rods of that day, and it made a large impression on us. So when about the end of that year or the beginning of the next a legacy put me in funds to acquire a replica of the 10-ft. Tournament rod, one of the first things I did was to order one, and I took it out to Bavaria on my September 1903 holiday and was so pleased with its perfor-mance that I let myself be persuaded to enter for the distance and accuracy event in the 1904 tournament. A badly damaged wrist prevented any success on the distance event, but I came second in the accuracy, only failing to win it because in the last and longest cast for accuracy a gust of wind caught my gut and fly just as they were being delivered and blew them off the marker.

Among the spectators was Mr. P.B. Mills, the senior member of the New York firm which sold the Leonard Tournament, and his son Eddie. I was introduced to them by Coggeshall, and, finding the young man anxious to try fishing on a chalk stream, I made interest with Mr. Irwin Cox to get the young man a day on the Itchen. He brought with him two rods of the Leonard make—one, which he used, a 9-ft. 5-oz. rod of fascinating action and the other a 2⅛-oz. piece of magic with which Priddis, the keeper, not only put out 23 yds. of line, but hooked and landed from a weedy stretch without using a landing net a 2-lb. 2-oz. trout in fine condition.

I was not fishing, contenting myself with following young Mills and providing him with appropriate flies, but his 9-ft. 5-oz. Leonard made such an impression on me that when next year a client wished to pay me a large sum in addition to my firm's costs, in recognition of a professional service, I declined the money as a benefit but expressed my willingness to accept as a compliment the best rod that money could buy, to be chosen by myself. He not only willingly accepted the plan but insisted on adding an appropriate reel and line to the gift.

It was a choice I never had reason to regret, and when in 1945 my trout fishing came to an end, I handed the rod and its one remaining top to my brother. The rod was as straight and as serviceable as on the day it was acquired, notwithstanding the hundreds of trout up to 3¼ lb. and numbers of grayling it had mastered in the forty years of its service.

Shocks and a Lesson

IN EARLY September 1891, having gone through a pretty strenuous time, I was badly run down when I started with an angling friend from the British Museum to spend ten days of my three weeks' annual holiday on the upper waters of the Yore; and at the expiration of that ten days I was not a little surprised to find that, thanks to the bracing moorland air and the good feeding provided by the good-natured landlady of the inn at which we stayed, I had put on no less than 13 lb. in weight. From there we planned to proceed to Winchester and to spend the remainder of our three weeks upon the Abbotts Barton stretch of the Itchen immediately above Winchester by the kind permission of the client who was the lessee of the water. I had been presented in 1887 with a copy of Halford's *Floating Flies and How to Dress Them*, and in 1889 with Halford's first edition of *Dry Fly Fishing in Theory and Practice*, and both of us, relatively inexperienced, looked on these immortal works as revelation from on high with all the authority of gospel truth.

We had heard on the day of our arrival in Winchester that the great man was putting up at The George and was nightly welcoming his worshippers at that hotel to hear him expound the pure and authentic gospel of the dry fly—which no one would dream of questioning. So that evening found us, after our meal, among the humble listeners. It came to our ears on that occasion that we were to have the great man's company on the Abbotts Barton water, the lessee having invited him for a week. With becoming reverence we listened to his words of wisdom until it became necessary that the session be broken up.

On the following day we were on the water a quarter of an hour or so before our mentor's arrival—taking the side stream, my friend above in the Ducks' Nest Spinney, I a couple of hundred yards further downstream, thus leaving the main river, the fishing of which was reputed the better, to the great man. He was not long behind us and presently we saw him casting on Winnel Water, the main river. Soon afterwards he crossed the meadow which divided the two streams and accosted me from the left bank of the side stream to advise us kindly on the fly to put up, and to make his advice clearer he cast his fly to light on the right bank of the side stream, having first ascertained that I had mounted a fly of George Holland's dressing, known as the quill marryat. He insisted that his fly, which was an india-rubber olive, was the right fly. My selection was based on little pale duns seen on the water. I took a look at his fly and was not a little shocked to see how coarse was the gut on which his fly was tied, but I was also too polite or timid to venture on such a comment.

We met at lunchtime and he inquired how I had done. I said two and a half brace. He had one trout only, but congratulated me civilly and offered to put me up for the Flyfishers' Club, then recently formed. Not expecting, despite my additional 13 lb. in ten days, to live long enough to make it worth while, I declined and did not in fact seek membership till the autumn of 1893, when a voyage to the Cape and back had gone a long way to re-establishing my health.

Halford only fished the Abbotts Barton length for three more days of this week, but just as I had been profoundly shocked to do

A FAVOURITE STRETCH

better than the great master did on the first day, I was fated to be similarly shocked on each of his three other days. Yet it encouraged me to rely most on my own observations and not to attach undue importance to authority. My friend, by the way, caught the biggest fish of the week (1 lb. 13 oz.), but it was his only catch.

At this period I had had little Itchen experience—perhaps three or four days each year since 1883, but for years afterwards I looked back on those four days whenever I was faced with the alternative of letting myself be guided by authority or going on my own wilful way, and I have seldom had grounds for regretting the lesson of September 1891.

Dr. H. Van Dyke

————◄o►————

IN 1917 I was acting secretary of the Flyfishers' Club in place of my younger brother who was on anti-aircraft service on the south coast, and, becoming aware that the Rev. Dr. Van Dyke, the eminent American angling author, was in London on his way back to America from Holland, where he had been his country's representative until the U.S.A. was drawn into the war, I obtained the leave of the committee to invite him to dine as a guest of the club, and was very gratified by his acceptance, also to find that he had picked up in St. Martin's Lane Mr. Irwin Cox's copy of *Minor Tactics of the Chalk Stream* which they had bought at Mr. Cox's sale of his great angling library. The meeting with the doctor led naturally to my inviting him to spend a Saturday with me by Itchen side and to his initiation into the methods of minor tactics as in course of its further development subsequent to its publication in 1910.

The day of his coming was fine and bright, but I was not favourably impressed by the learned doctor's split cane of American make, which struck me as unduly limber and lacking in backbone.

Well, I'm Damned!

————◀o▶————

MY FRIEND Fleur de Lys, one of the little Itchen syndicate, had told me of his intention to acquire a 9-ft. 5-oz. Leonard split cane to match my little miracle of the same make presented to me in 1905; and one day after his rod had become due I got down to the Itchen half an hour later than usual, and, reaching the hut, I joined Fleur de Lys, wielding his new rod and diligently casting an accurate fly to a trout of 1 lb. 13 oz. which was rising steadily near the right bank of the main river 25 or 30 yds. above the hut. Seeing me, he called, "See whether you can do anything with the damned fish; I have been casting to him for the last half-hour and he keeps on rising—but won't look at me." "That the new Leonard?" I asked. "Yes, try it," said he. I took the rod and ran the line and gut through my hand and looked at the fly, a very nicely tied red quill. "Aren't you going to change it?" said he. "What's the matter with a red quill?" I asked, and put the fly into the air. I made just one cast and the fly lit on the stream side of the trout four or five inches below his right eye. As it lit, the trout turned its head and sucked on the fly. I set the hook and called to Fleur de Lys. "There, take your rod!" "Why?" "Your fish." Drawing in his breath, he took the rod. "Well, I'm damned!" said he, accepting it.

It is well worth knowing that a fly lighting just behind his eye will often take a trout which would refuse it coming to him down-stream from above.

Windy Ways

————◄o►————

AN EARLY experience on the Abbotts Barton water led me to realise that a violent gale sufficient to blow every newly hatched fly off the water was by no means fatal to the hope of killing a good fish, though not a rise could be seen to attract a cast from one end of the water to the other. The first incident to give me this idea occurred on the short stretch of the main stream running from McCaskie's Corner on the west to the small paddock behind the little church of Winnal St. Magdalen on the east. There was a fresh gale blowing from the south across the river, making quite a ruffle under the left bank on the north side. Just what possessed me to knot on a winged fly on a No. 3 hook I am unable to say. There was not a hatched fly to be seen, but no sooner had my fly lit on the ruffled patch of water under the far bank than it was grabbed with a savage swish by a strong trout which presently pulled down the spring balance to record a weight of 3 lb. 1 oz. I had not at the time of the incident sufficient experience to follow up this hint— and I took no other trout that day.

There are not many occasions on that water when conditions resembled the above-described incident, but I recall one queer June day much later in date when the grayling had multiplied so as to become a nuisance. Overnight at a point just above McCaskie's Corner the trout had been taking something big under water and it occurred to me that they were taking newly hatched toads carried into the stream through breaks in the east bank letting off the flood waters from the swamped meadow in the east. Neither I nor my guest had any lures dressed with intent to represent a small toad, but I put on a sedge of a dressing which I hoped might be near enough to do the trick. Sure enough it did, both my guest and I catching trout each with small toads in its crop. I left the fly on its cast and, coming down on the following week-end, I found the stretch from the boathouse and luncheon hut ripped by a violent downstream gale. Though no fly was to be seen, small fish were flopping away freely. The wind was too high to cast against and so I started to fish downstream without changing my fly. In the straight I caught and landed twenty-six small grayling and put back

a dozen small trout. At the foot of it I remembered having seen a big trout in the corner where the stream turns south and despatched the sedge fly to his address. One cast was enough—he grabbed the fly. The trout proved to weigh 2 lb. 13 oz. As the grayling continued to rise in the next short stretch I went on fishing across and down, and after adding seven more to my score I saw a good trout turn under water as if to scour himself on the bottom. He followed the sedge fly half-way across the water before taking it. Weight 2 lb. 6 oz. After that I knocked off.

A final incident occurred in 1938, almost the last time I fished the water. I came out for the evening, to find the surface torn with a strong gale. Nothing seemed to be rising, but I recalled a three-pounder that I had seen on my last visit, under the far bank opposite to McCaskie's Corner. I had on my cast a No. 4 wood-cock and orange sedge, and, though I had little hope, I resolved to go down to the corner before turning in. To my delight, a little way below the point opposite to McCaskie's Corner I spotted a little area about a yard square in which three fish were feeding greedily as if to B.W.O. I did not, however, change my fly, but let the current drag it across the area above-mentioned, when it was grabbed by the biggest of the three trout. He was 3 lb. 1 oz., but his removal did not disturb the other two. Presently I was leading number two by the nose—2 lb. 9 oz. Yet number three fed on until he took the sedge as guilelessly as number one and two. Weight 1 lb. 13 oz. Then I called it a day and went in.

Fisherman Hut—Naboth's Vineyard

THE HUT referred to here is not that Piscatoribus Sacrum which long stood at the spot where the main stream and the side stream come closest together at the lower end of the Ducks' Nest Spinney—but is on the downstream end of Old Barge—south of the road crossing the Itchen Valley.

In that period Mr. Cox's lease of the Abbotts Barton fishing sternly forbade Sunday fishing, but the kindness of H.E. Gribble (in 1896 president of the Flyfishers' Club) gave me several Sundays with him on the little stretch of the river which ran between the road above-mentioned and the point where Logie Stream discharged near the gasworks into the head of the St. Cross length, then being fished by F.M. Halford and Edgar Williamson. There were also some opportunities afforded by streams let off from the canal-like length which ran under St. Catherine's on Abbotts Barton—but it made much more of a week-end to share the Sunday morning and afternoon on that tiny little bit of water. It was immensely generous of Gribble to share it with me, for we seldom got more than a brace between us. Below we looked down to St. Cross Mill. Williamson and Halford had not only that but the long stretch below reaching to Shawford. But it was not enough for them, for there soon came a season when Gribble told me he no longer had that little bit, for it had been let during the winter to Williamson.

The Advantages of a Serious Handicap[1]

———◄o►———

I N AN article which appeared in *The Field* of 5th December 1943, under the title "Right Under Our Eyes", Dr. N.B. McCaskie wrote:

"In all the annals of fishing I know of no feat of pure observation to equal Mr. Skues' differentiation between the rise of a nymphing and a surface-feeding trout. We had all watched them at it a hundred times, but he really saw what we had only been looking at. Those who do not know of his discovery—and they are still more than a few—find it hard to believe, and feel that they are being asked to discredit the evidence of their own eyes. When we tell them that the fish which they see rising is really feeding under water, they think that we are offering rather a feeble excuse for our failure to catch it with a floating fly, and privately rate us as very indifferent anglers who have not even noticed that the sun is too bright or that there is thunder in the air. If we are inclined to admire our own powers of observation when we have counted three setae in a dun's tail, it is well to remember many efforts thwarted and opportunities missed before Mr. Skues pointed out what we could very well have seen for ourselves."

[1] Reprinted from *The Anglers' Club Bulletin*, vol. xxv, no. 1, by kind permission of the proprietors.

Even if I had not known that—following an operation performed on my left eye when I was nine, the right eye is the only effective one, the left eye being unable to distinguish anything in detail—I should never have ventured to pitch my claim as high as Dr. N.B. McCaskie has put it for me. Nevertheless, for a good many years, it has been something of a puzzle to me that so many anglers with normal vision (including men fishing crack waters of Test and Itchen and other first-rate chalk streams) have failed to realise what a large proportion of the rises to be seen are rises to nymphs or other subaqueous diet, when to my one-eyed vision no floating insect had been taken. Latterly I have even ventured to speculate on the question whether my one-eyed vision might not have been responsible for letting me see what so many missed.

Halford wrote (the chapter entitled "Studies of Fish Feeding" in *Dry Fly Fishing in Theory and Practice*):

"Sometimes fish, when feeding on larvae and nymphae, rise quietly and do not move about much from place to place, and under these circumstances it is almost impossible to distinguish the apparent from the bona fide rises, except by watching intently the surface of the water with the view of making certain that the winged duns are being taken."

But he then went on to illustrate this passage by recounting an occasion in which he shows he was deceived, for he offered the trout in succession a series of several floaters, eventually, after an hour or more, getting him at dusk with a small silver sedge, and then found, as the result of an autopsy, that the fish contained not a single winged fly.

At the billiard table my monocular vision has undoubtedly been a great disadvantage, especially when I took trouble with a shot; yet at times, when I just trusted my one eye and let myself go without worrying about it, I have brought off a sensational success. On one occasion I found a friend playing a practice game of slosh by himself. He called to me. "Did you ever see such a position? There is not a single ball on the board which will go." His white cue ball was up near the upper left-hand pocket, the green was on its spot at the left end of the D, and the black lay almost directly in between.

I looked at the board and said, "I think the green would go."

"Rot," he said.

"Well," I replied, "that is not too polite, but I still think green would go."

"I bet you five bob you couldn't make it," he said.

"I am the world's worst billiards player," I replied, "but I don't mind trying. Not that if I fail it would prove me wrong."

I took the cue and almost without aiming I sent the white past the black without touching it and chipped the green into the bottom left-hand pocket without it touching either cushion. My friend made an imprudent prophecy as to his eternal future and insisted on paying me the five shillings, though I protested I had not betted. (Incidentally, he never forgave me.)

My theory is that, being one-eyed, I was able to see that there was a straight line between the white and the green which would just bring the former to the edge of the latter without touching the black, and that for the purpose of that shot my monocular vision could be more accurate than my friend's normal eyesight. The analogy of a rifle or gun shot screwing up one eye when aiming occurred to me. Being one-eyed, I had no need to close one eye.

Latterly I have wondered at times whether in spotting the nature of rises my monocular vision may not have had advantages over normal two-eyed eyesight. For several successive seasons in the last century it had intrigued me that so often it was impossible to see the floating fly which I had been taught to infer the trout took, and it was not till some time in the 'nineties, when I found green nymphs in the mouth of a trout, that I was able to tumble to the explanation.

After that, though I frequently looked in the mouths of trout, I seldom found either flies or nymphs: I hated the messy and nauseous business of an autopsy, and did not find that a teaspoon brought up much. So I lacked models of nymphs to imitate, until ultimately I discovered that a marrow scoop brought up the stomach contents entire. Till then, though I had imitated several nymphs, I had not been able to make the progress in precise representation of them which I was afterwards able to make.

Human Angling Mascots[1]

————◄○►————

I S IT, I wonder, a common experience among anglers that the
approach or presence of some particular person at the waterside
has almost invariably coincided with the catching of trout, while
the approach or presence of others is as invariably attended by failure to catch?

There was, for instance, on the length of the Itchen which I so
long frequented, a keeper whose advice on flies or methods was
never tendered, for the good reason that he was quite ignorant on
the subject. Yet I always welcomed his coming to me by the waterside, for he almost always seemed to arrive just in time to net for
me a good trout, or else I got one during the brief period of his stay.
The other keeper's presence worked in quite a different way, for
while on rare occasions he came up in time to officiate with the
landing net, yet when he was in close attendance it was the rarest
thing for me to catch anything.

In another instance the elderly wife of an angling friend, who at
times accompanied her husband and me on angling vacations,
would at times sit on the bank behind us and read a book, or knit,
or crochet. But as soon as she did so I would be catching trout—

[1] Reprinted from *The Anglers' Club Bulletin* vol. xxv, no. 2, June 1946, by kind
permission of the proprietors.

THE SITE OF "PISCATORIBUS SACRUM"

lots of them, often twice as fast as her good man, though I followed him over the same stretch of river.

On another occasion I recall a friend wanted to cross a plank bridge under which lay a trout to which I had been casting for twenty minutes. "Hold on a sec.," I said, "till I catch this trout." "Do you want me to wait a fortnight?" he said. "Only two chucks," I replied, and at the second chuck the trout came up and fastened. Then my friend made a confident forecast of his eternal future, and walked the plank.

In the late August of the very last season before he resigned from the syndicate I had had a disastrous day without a single trout to my credit, when at about three in the afternoon he came down the bank. I was casting to a big and obstinate fish which was rising intermittently, until he hailed me, when the trout sipped in my little spent pale watery spinner, and he was just in time to dish out for me a 2¾-lb. fish. The same evening I was caught in a torrential downpour which lasted from seven till nine. My friend came out just after it was all over, just as I began to fish, and had found one of the only two risers I saw that evening, and he reached me as I netted out a trout of 3¼ lb., making, with the trout of the afternoon, the biggest brace I ever had out of that water. That brought my tale of trout of 2 lb. and upwards for that season to nine and a half brace, and I wanted badly to make it ten brace, never having had more than eight and a half brace before. I was on the water at ten next morning, but did nothing, until, a little after eleven, my friend turned up, just in time to net out my twentieth two-pounder for me.

I did not see him again on the water, and though I had two more August week-ends (I don't fish the length in September) I got no more two-pounders.

In none of these cases can I give, or even suggest, any reason for the strange persistent chain of coincidences. But there they are. And I would be interested to hear whether any other anglers have had similar experiences.

My Grossest Piece of Tactlessness[1]

————◀o▶————

THE INCIDENT I have to relate occurred in June 1913, long before I retired from the practice of the law. I had to get the signature of a client to an elaborate and urgent agreement and to get him sworn to a no less elaborate and urgent affidavit in connection with it. The client was the lessee of an attractive length of the Itchen on which for years past he had generously given me standing fishing leave, and, being down by the water with guests for a week, he had to be caught at the water side. My train reached Winchester at four o'clock. I rushed into the city and secured a Commissioner for Oaths, arranging for him to meet me on the river at the fishing hut at five-thirty. Then on to the keeper's to collect my 9-ft. Leonard, my linen bag with damper, gut and fly-box and my landing net. Thence through the meadows to the hut to meet my client and to explain to him the agreement and take him through his affidavit before the arrival of the Commissioner for Oaths. The Commissioner was before time and the business was dispatched by the half-hour, which also saw the arrival at the hut of the two guests who had spent the day fishing with the client. Alas, the creels of both were "toom", and the client's catch for the day—a bright and

[1] Reprinted from the *Journal of the Flyfishers' Club* vol. xxxiv, no. 134, summer, 1945, by kind permission of the proprietors.

a hot day—was limited to one small grayling. All three were tired, but the client said, "We are having a cold dinner in the hut at six-thirty. Now you run along and see what you can make of it, and come back for dinner at six-thirty."

Apparently conditions must have changed, for the trout showed little hesitation about accepting my red spinner, and I brought in two and a half brace of quite nice sizeable fish, all caught within 200 yds. of the hut.

The hut stood those days at a point where the two branches of the Itchen, which water those meadows, come close together and hard by a wooden trunk built to take a stream from the main across the side stream to water the eastern meadows below the Ducks' Nest Spinney. Above the trunk in the side stream were the string of fish, reputedly uncatchable, though perennially rising, known as the "Aunt Sallies". (For the trunk see frontispiece to *Sidelines, Sidelights and Reflections*. For the haunt of the Aunt Sallies see illustration facing p. 103 of *Sidelines, Sidelights and Reflections*.)

The meal was over when one of the guests, an elderly colonel, looking out of the window, exclaimed, "There they go, those damned Aunt Sallies. Nobody can catch them." Whether it was due to the client's whisky or my afternoon's success, or to a combination of the two, I know not, but I said to the client, "Do you mind if I have a go at them?" "Go on, dear boy," he said, "and we will look through the window and laugh." Picking up my rod and net, I crawled into the trunk, and cast my fly, unchanged, to the lowest of the risers, promptly hooked him and netted him out as he sought to run under the trunk. The next fish took with equal simplicity and was safely netted. The third rose close to the bank, and a not quite accurate cast put the fly over a small snag projecting from the bank, and I had to break the point. Another fish, however, was putting up beyond the first tree on the right bank, and, clambering out of the trunk on to the Ducks' Nest Spinney, I covered him with a new fly of the same pattern and had him out. My watch then showed that I had to run to catch my train (about seven-thirty) back to London. So bidding farewell to my client and his guests, I made off with my four brace of trout, to leave the rod and gear at the keeper's and reach the station just as the London train was puffing in.

An eminent barrister, since a judge, who knew the water and to whom I related the story, said, "Well, that is the grossest piece of tactlessness I ever heard of." But I would ask what else could I do with my fish? I could hardly humiliate my host by offering him fish from his own water—emphasising his lack of success. Still less could I have offered them to the two guests, leaving my host out.

What is the verdict?

Whose Trout?

————◄o►————

I HAVE already expressed my views on the growing tendency in the little syndicate of four members that fished the stretch of Itchen of which I write to restrict the admission of guests to fish the water, and ultimately, in the middle 'thirties, much to my disgust, the only way in which it was possible to entertain a friend on it was to invite him to share one's rod. I had, and thank goodness still have, a friend (C.L.C.) to whom this restriction was not wholly a penance, because he was a devout admirer of my rod—a lovely little 9-ft. 5-oz. Leonard, dating back to 1905, which he styled W.B.R., which, being interpreted, means World's Best Rod, and so it fell to him one Saturday in June to motor over from a neighbouring valley and a village which had sheltered Izaak Walton in his old age, and to meet me on the middle of our two-mile stretch. I had entered the meadows from the bottom of the length and had been detained for a while at a bend known as Mac's Corner, where the trout had the exasperating habit of proving nearly, but very seldom quite, 3 lb.—and on the occasion in question each of the brace I extracted from that curve ran true to form—2 lb. 15 oz.

However, that was good enough to reconcile me, when I met my friend on the middle of the stretch about eleven o'clock, to surrendering my W.B.R. to him, with the cast and the midget nymph which had done the trick with my brace—and I soon had the satisfaction of seeing my friend leading by the nose to my ready landing net a quite pleasant two-pounder. Then I was able to tell him that a few yards further upstream at a bend there was suspected to be a quite impossible three-pounder: and not long after I was privileged to see the W.B.R.'s top go up and the W.B.R. make the curve of beauty and to hear my friend exclaim, "Got him!" It was some minutes before he got a glimpse of his fish and exclaimed, "By George, I believe he's a four-pounder!" It was some minutes more before he could turn the trout and persuade him to head downstream. All, however, seemed to be going well till the trout was brought close under our bank, when he took a scare and tore the line off the shrieking reel and, with a wrench under the far bank, kicked free.

I do not recall that anything outstanding marked the rest of our day together.

Two or three weeks later I was on the river about a hundred yards below the scene of the tragedy narrated, when, near the top of a straight run of about 300 yds. of river, I saw under the far bank (the left) a small raft of cut weed collected by some underwater obstruction. Watching the spot as a likely one, I presently observed the surface broken by a tiny swirl which I had no difficulty in attributing to the absorption of a nymph. Taking the hint, I dropped my nymph with an 00 Pennell sneck in it an inch or two below the raft of cut weed and had the immediate satisfaction of seeing the floating gut drawn under as by some adhesion and, on raising the tip of the W.B.R., finding that I was into something solid. My usual experience with trout hooked under that far bank (and I had had them up to and just over 3 lb.) was that they could generally be persuaded to cross over and come under my bank and be played and killed there. But this fish was not having any. Nothing I could do would bring him across, and for the entire three hundred yards to Mac's Corner, though he came downstream, he bored stubbornly under the left bank. At Mac's Corner, however, there is a right-angled turn of the river to the east with the push of the current across to the right bank, and here, with the aid of that push, I succeeded at length in bringing that stubborn trout under my bank. But he turned upstream immediately and forced his way, still under my bank, for a hundred yards or more before I could again turn him and lead him foot by foot to a little bare patch at the top of Mac's Corner, when for the first time I got a view of his proportions. From that point I resolved that the battle *must* be finished there. But again and again, as I led him towards the waiting net, he sheered off, still keeping his balance. But at last, at the umpteenth shot, I had the net under him and drew him ashore.

Was he, could he be a four-pounder? It was years since one had been taken on that stretch. The priest having performed his office, I fixed the hook of my spring balance into the trout's jaw, and was delighted to see it pull down to 4 lb. 3 or 4 oz. But, alas, it thought better of it and reverted to 3 lb. 14 oz., where it stayed. Still, it was the biggest trout I had ever had from the Itchen in over fifty years, though I had two or three times seen and twice had hooked bigger. But the regretful reflection assailed me, "Was it my friend's lost fish?" Hooked a short stretch below the spot where C.L.C.'s loss had occurred, it was unlikely that another fish of that size would have been so near.

A curious feature of the kill was that though the trout was hooked in the upper jaw the hook had worn through that jaw and secured a tight grip on the lower jaw.

The Swan's Sense of Decency[1]

————◄○►————

AT McCASKIE's Corner, where my friend McCaskie has lured some excellent trout to their doom, the Itchen comes down in a straight run of, say, 300 yds. from the north, turning at McCaskie's Corner, at a right angle, and running due east for a hundred yards or more to the paddock abutting on the churchyard of Winnal St. Magdalen and then turning south again for maybe another hundred yards to the most northerly buildings of Winchester. The land on the east side of the river was marsh land, the haunt of coot, moorhen, mallard, teal and tufted duck, and at the point opposite to McCaskie's Corner a pair of swans had established a huge nest, barring passage to anyone along the east bank. Upstream, just around the corner above their nest, is a spot under the east bank which for all the years I have known the water has been the haunt of good trout—just a longish cast from the west bank.

Well, as I came up the river on the west bank on that May morning a trout put up in the expected spot, and I prepared to cast. I had seen and passed the cob swan rooting weeds from the river bed some yards below, but, being on the far side from his nest, I felt no reason to apprehend his interference. Yet no sooner had I let out

[1] Reprinted from *Angling*, vol. vii, no. 32, July-Sept. 1944, by kind permission of the proprietors.

DUCKS' NEST SPINNEY

nearly enough line to reach my fish (note the word "my") than I became aware that the bird was surging upstream under forced draught and had almost reached a point directly between me and the fish.

There was just time, I thought, for one cast. But as my Tup's Indispensable alighted I perceived that the line had fallen across the swan's back between his neck and wings. I saw also that the trout had risen, and, striking quietly, I hooked it. The rush of the fish straightened the line across the swan's back, lifting it, but not high enough to escape ruffling the bird's neck plumage. He turned and cursed me, and for several minutes I played the fish with the swan surging to and fro between it and me.

The moment came when the trout seemed ready for the net, but first the swan had to be fended off. I picked up a handy clod of earth with grass growing in it and lobbed it luckily into the middle of the swan's back. It drove him off for the necessary moment, and I dipped out the trout (2 lb. 6 oz.) while the swan sheered off, still raging and swearing.

That, however, was not the end of the matter. The following week-end, coming up the meadows on the west bank I reached a point just downstream of the southerly corner of the paddock above mentioned, when I thought I spotted a suspicious movement under a willow on the east bank. I had put on experimentally a newly devised pattern of iron-blue nymph, and after several offers thought I spotted another suspicious movement under the willow. The next moment I was battling with *some* trout, and felt quite happy.

Not so happy, however, when a moment later I espied the cob swan surging downstream again under forced draught, obviously bent on intervention. I played the trout as hard as I dared and actually had it under my rod point when the swan arrived. He stood on his tail on the water within striking distance of the fish, and flapped his wings and cursed me savagely by all the gods in the swanny Pantheon without ever repeating himself. I was afraid from his behaviour that he would strike the line with his wings or the fish off the 000 hook with his beak. Just in time I espied a loose half-brick and with a second lucky shot lobbed it on to the swan's back. Snarling with rage, he drew off, long enough to let me get my net under the fish and hoist it ashore—3¼ lb. The swan was left cursing.

You would have thought that after that relations would be strained between the swan and me. Not a bit of it! Within a few weeks he and his wife with a team of cygnets were, as boldly and persistently as a swarm of Neapolitan beggars, impudently demanding to share my sandwiches. No, I do not consider the swan a self-respecting bird.

Five Successive Saturday Evenings
or
Five Times Seven

————◄o►————

THE YEAR 1916 was a great one for the B.W.O. Fine evenings and good hatches and my week-ends, with Sundays barred, gave me a unique succession of good baskets (seven good trout in each) all caught on an orange quill cast upstream under the right bank on one short straight stretch of about 100 yds. of the main river running from the boathouse at the point where it most nearly approaches the side stream down to its turn southward. They were fighters from fighting stock and I did not lose a fish or a fly on any one of those five amazing evenings. This sequence confirmed me more than any other experience in my faith in the orange quill as a killer on evenings when the B.W.O. are hatching. The story of my dressing of the merits of the orange quill of an evening when blue-winged olive are hatching is told in *Sidelines, Sidelights and Reflections*, my third book.

The Green-Winged Olive

ONE BRIGHT but cold Saturday afternoon in an April early in the century I got down to Winchester to join two friends who had gone down earlier to fish the Abbotts Barton stretch of the Itchen, and after a visit to the keeper's to collect my 10-ft. Leonard Tournament split cane, with reel and landing net and bag, I strolled across the new city park and got a boatman at the south-east corner of the park to ferry me across the side stream to the narrow slip of land which divides it from the water called Swift Lake.

There was a light cold downstream wind from the north-east, but what struck me immediately was the fact that every little bay under both banks of the side stream was closely packed with a flotilla of upwinged duns. I netted out a few and found that every one of the flies had a vivid green wing and that the body of each was a rich brown olive with pale greenish yellow at the segments. It seemed to me remarkable that notwithstanding the tremendous size of the hatch not a trout was taking the slightest notice of these flies, and I had to walk up till I almost reached the culverts in the bank through which the Red Hole and Swift Lake are fed before I saw a fish move. Then I saw underneath the west bank of the side stream a nice sizeable trout which was cruising under a flotilla of duns and now and then tilting his muzzle to suck in something, but never a green olive. I could not see what he was taking, but tied on an iron blue quill at a venture. It lit near him, but he took no notice at first until the stream began to drag the line, then he followed promptly and sucked in the fly, disregarding the drag. Having performed the obsequies and put the trout in the bag, I moved on up, and I had to pass the city bathing place before I found another fish, but between the bathing place and the long spinney which runs across the meadows to join the side stream I found two trout which behaved exactly like number one taking my iron blue and joining it in the bag.

Then my two friends put in an appearance, disappointed and entirely blank, and together we drifted down to the boatman's corner and were ferried across to the park and the keeper's.

Years before I had found in an old fly book patterns of a starling-winged dun, the wings dyed a bright green, from which I had deduced that there must be a type of blue dun with green wings. But never till that day had I come across one, and then it was in millions, and never again during the fifty-six years I fished the Itchen either on that or any other water have I seen a green-winged olive.

A Soft Thing[1]

———◄○►———

I T WAS on the edge of spinner time that I came out after tea on an
August Saturday afternoon and made my way up the east bank
of the Itchen to a bend which runs almost due west to east, where
it was my purpose to await the early stages of the evening rise. I had
hardly "attained my objective", when I marked a rise at the tail of
a bunch of cut weed which was bunched against my own bank. It
was a soft rise, but definite enough; but I was too near.

Dropping cautiously into the tall reeds and willow-herb, I
retreated a few paces, and thence I delivered my seal's fur-bodied
red spinner to the address. It fell a couple of feet further into the
stream than I intended, but it was of no consequence, for the fly
had not travelled a foot before my rod was bending to the plunge
of a grayling whose inches indicated a weight of close on 2 lb. He
was in due course conducted ashore, and was followed by a brace
of his fellows of about 1½ lb. each out of the next three rises spotted on the same length. It looked as if the evening was going to
prove a soft thing for me. But it is never safe to count on the willingness of grayling as any clue to the disposition of the trout, or
vice versa.

[1] Reprinted from an article in the *Fishing Gazette*, by kind permission of the
proprietors.

By the time I had reached the bend (and the reach was little more than 100 yds. long) I had seen no other rise, and the weather, which for four and twenty days had been blazing, began to show definite signs of breaking up. The wind, however, what little there was, came from the south-east, and I thought there would be little beyond a spit, and that soon over. So I pushed my way through the masses of willow-herb, often topping my head by a foot or two, and made for the first gap at which I might hope to find the river accessible.

As luck would have it, I came out at a spot where the weeds were growing out of the river for eight or ten yards from the bank. On the outer edge lay a trout something better than a pound, obviously waiting for the rise to begin. I offered him the spinner, and it fell just beyond and behind him. He turned languidly, followed it down for a couple of yards, then opened his mouth as if to take it, thought better of it, and returned to his station. Of a second offer he took no notice, so I decided to try him with a sedge of small size. When, however, I looked up from knotting on my fly, he was gone. The rain, however, was not. Still, it was not heavy, and I decided to push on. Yet, by way of precaution, before pushing through more masses of willow-herb, I decided to slip on my light mackintosh, and soon had reason to be glad I had done so. For no sooner was I definitely committed to that eastern bank, with acres of marsh and bog between me and real dry land, than the rain began to come down with a will. I took it, however, in good part, for my waders protected my legs and my mackintosh my body, and only my hat took a soaking.

When I started along that bank, however, I had little notion how the tall growths cut one off from access to the river, and how little of it was fishable from that side with a nine-footer. Here and there I saw an occasional rise under the western bank where the current set but, generally speaking, I was cut off by the growth on the bank from casting to most of the fish, and the three which I did succeed in covering in the next half-mile would have nothing to do with me. Then I reached a more open bend with the current under my own bank. Here I found a couple of grayling dimpling, but they would have no truck with me. My gauze net showed that some black gnats were going down; also a little dark spinner, and an occasional sedge. I put up a little dark rusty spinner in the hope of finding a trout in one of the familiar corners in an accommodating humour but there was none moving, and I was again committed to battle with the marsh herbage, and by the time I arrived at the choice length where the current ran deep under my own bank, my mackintosh was as wet with sweat inside as with rain from the willow-herb, the sedges and the reeds on the outside, and still I was troutless.

To add to my discomfiture, the wind, instead of dying down, as it should have done, began to get up, and soon was blowing briskly from the south, bringing with it torrents of rain, which my light mackintosh was not sufficient entirely to repel, and I began to feel an unpleasant sensation of cold in my elbows. Gladly would I have gone in, but it was still three-quarters of an hour to the time when the keeper was due at the opposite bank to punt over and fetch me. There was nothing for it but to stick it out. But here again I found the rain-laden willow-herb higher and denser than ever, and I had to push through masses of it before I could get a sight of the river at all.

At length I came to a place where the growth was different and reached little above my waist, and here I stood in the rain for the best part of half an hour while the dark made rapid progress. The trend of the river here was from north-east to south-west, and under my bank there was thus a little shelter from the wind.

Presently the rain thinned to a drizzle and I became aware of something that looked like a recurring heavy drip in the water under my bank. There was nothing to drip from, however, and, watching, I made up my mind that it was a trout and that it was taking spinners. How I tied on an orange seal's-fur (sherry) spinner in that light with my hat pouring torrents over my hands I do not know, but I made a sound job of it. Seven, eight, or nine times I covered the trout with a line not seven yards long from the tip of my rod, and then there was a sudden jar as a most indignant trout took the point in the extreme tip of his lip. He tore almost all my line off in the first rush. I could not follow him, as I did not want to disturb what was left to me of open bank, so I had to let him run. But presently I had him back under the rod point and dished him out—1 lb. 10 oz.

Meanwhile, the rain had ceased and a curious threatening glare showed upon the sky and reflected on the surface. It enabled me to detect another quiet dimple almost on the edge of the ruffled water. One offer was enough. I struck at the dimple and felt a hard jar: a good fish sprang wildly into the air, and my line came back to me. There was not another twenty yards of open bank left to me, and I was determined not to commit myself to further battle with the willow-herb. So I watched carefully and, peering into the dusk, made out just one other riser under my own bank. The spinner was his game, too, and presently he took his place in my bag, adding 1 lb. 3 oz. to the burden on my shoulders, but taking quite that weight off my spirits.

There was nothing more to be seen moving, so I reeled up and started to force my way back through a couple of yards to the place where the keeper was waiting with the punt to ferry me over to land that was land, and a short way back to my inn. And as I crouched drenched in the slushing punt I reflected that things had come about differently from my anticipation, and that it was not the evening, but I that had turned out to be *a soft thing.*

Diary of an Itchen Week[1]

————◄o►————

Saturday, 15th July 1911.

ARRIVED TOO late to put up rod. Too late even to stroll down to the mill-head and see the rings widening along the outer bend.

Sunday, 16th July.

Out at eight. Strolled round to the saw-mill and found trout already busy in the head, lining up along the edge of the bend where the strength of the stream runs. Watched minutely through Goerz Trieder monocular for twenty minutes, but never fly on the water, though the fish were rising regularly several times a minute. Every now and then the upper limb of the trout's tail peeped through the widening ring as he descended. This suggested spinners, but a careful study of the surface showed no sign of a spinner. Sunday being a *dies non*, went and sat on slope commanding higher reaches, and saw more fortunately placed anglers setting out with their rods. This is near the end of second week of drought. Very hot and sunny. River low, weeds high, and giant rushes so grown as to be a nuisance in places. This is a great year for mullein; tall spikes

---

[1] Reprinted from an article in the *Fishing Gazette*, by kind permission of the proprietors. It is included because Theodore Gordon, the great American angler, wrote of it when it appeared in the *Fishing Gazette* of 5th August 1911, that he would like more of the same kind.

in great clusters. Ragwort also in huge patches; toad-flax, both yellow and lilac, in great profusion. Never saw so many green-veined white butterflies; they seem to have meeting and mating places in damp spots; could have covered two dozen in one spot with landing-net. Cows up to their middles in river, or capering round with dinky little kinks in their tails. Horses, too, pestered with flies. But for a brisk breeze from west to south-west mitigating the heat, it would be unendurable. Glad I had foresight to order in large supply of syphons. After lunch, trout still busy in mill-head. Still no sign of fly, but one rod's gillie said his master had done well enough with No. 1 Whitchurch. Royal sunset. Dispute whether red enough to ensure fine tomorrow; wind prescribed.

Monday, 17th July.

Could not sleep; up at five and out in meadows. Took rod, in case. Fine and sunny, but air close; no dew on grass. Trout already under banks, but mostly in places where weeds prevented flow of water, and quite unapproachable. Broad banks of ribbon weed for 15 ft. to 20 ft. on either side, often loaded with piles of cut weed sent on from upper waters. Found one trout in running water and got him with a small landrail and hare's-ear sedge. After breakfast met Keeper Humfry, who says lower end of side stream has been cut, and that I was in for week of weed-cutting. Used expression designed to meet the case. Just my luck! Sun hot and high, wind veering west to south-west, enough to temper extreme of heat but not put up much ruffle. Found trout rising steadily in main, putting up noses as if taking surface food. But no fly to be seen. One fish came short to small No. 1 Whitchurch, and was pricked with Pope's Nondescript 00. No spinners or fly on water. Used small-meshed fly-net and caught pale-brown nymph. Matched it from my nymph box, and tackled trout rising in bays on opposite bank. In course of morning killed two brace and lost three others, besides mistiming one or two; delivered nymph wet by means of switch cast. Not a winged fly in any fish killed. Returned one trout. Evening rise in two parts. First, small fly or spinner (could not get on to right pattern, and continued trying too long). Then blue-winged olive. At length awoke to situation, and put up orange quill on No. 1 hook and killed brace of bankers. Home to interview syphon.

Tuesday, 18th July.

Cooler; wind north-west, fresh. Again no fly, but no feeding fish could be found except a brace which showed once or twice near some cut weed lodged against the west bank. Got both with small landrail and hare's-ear sedge, and fluked another (unfortunately unsizeable) against next weed patch. This was silvery, like sea-trout, and in pink of condition.

Doubted whether he were not a sea trout. Never saw any fish quite so bright in Itchen before. In afternoon found long yellow fish on gravelly exposed shallow in side irrigation carrier, and offered sedge. To surprise he took it; but, alas, kicked off in first run. No more good all day. In evening hooked and lost nice fish on jenny spinner, and killed good brace on large orange quill. Found glow-worm on railway line on way home.

Wednesday, 19th July.
Went to look for long yellow friend on gravelly shallow. Presented petition. Reply: "Too poor and know too much." But got rather smaller fish a few yards on. Lady angler on water about ten. Weather cloudy and heavy, but with bright intervals. No rise till twelve-fifteen, when found two good fish, in main nymphing in bay in weeds on east side. Gave them brown nymph as before with switch cast. Each boiled at it and missed, and declined to bid again. Luncheon interval. Afterwards a few half-hearted risers in main, but nothing fastened except unsizeable grayling. All over by three. Nothing moving in the ditches and carriers. Drying irrigation ditches full of young thrushes and blackbirds. Weasels get lots of them. Smelt weasel about in several places, but saw none. Amused at determined efforts of black-headed bunting to lure me from neighbourhood of nest by pretending to be unable to get away. Several kingfishers about. About seven-thirty, in shelter of spinney by side stream, found trout modestly rehearsing early evening rise by himself close under opposite bank. Offered jenny spinner dry with switch cast and got him first time of asking. Crossed to east bank of main. Got brace of grayling with jenny spinner, and made up three and a half brace with orange quill. Another glow-worm on railway line tonight. Could hear young screech-owls calling for food from three different quarters on my tramp home-along.

SWIFT LAKE

Speculate why I never get caught up at night. In day, dock, figwort, and thistles, and an odious little plant whose name I do not know, are always hanging my line up and causing me to exercise Christian patience, but at night I can go on casting over them to bankers by the hour, landing my fly with 18 in. or so of gut on the water, rest of line on bank, and never get a hang-up that is not easily released. Same rod on each occasion—9-ft. 5-oz. Leonard.

Then how does one judge distance at night so as to cast almost to an inch? Is it by the weight of the line out? I am sure to cast more accurately at night than by day.

At night, when one knocks off, the life in the air is a wonder. Big ghost swifts, male and female (the white and yellow bustards of the north), and an innumerable array of moths and sedges are buzzing around all intent on the business of life. Consider staying out for sedge rise for once.

Thursday, 20th July.

Blazing hot again. Wind westerly in morning. Round to south in afternoon. Again no rise of dun beyond a very few pale wateries, but by dint of remembering where good fish lay picked up a nice brace on the main by dropping red sedge in pockets in weeds, and caught a third trout with same fly in fast-running carrier. In evening caught brace of grayling (one about 2½ lb.) to red quill, and made up four brace with a leash of good trout to the orange quill. Blue-winged olive rise very suddenly over. Fish much shyer in water where weed-cutting done than where weeds left. Tried big sedge in vain for half-hour. Obviously do not understand game.

Friday, 21st July.

Saw weed-cutting finished last night on the side streams. Drowner tells me it begins on upper half of main today. So go down to bottom of main where it has been cut longest. Arrive at bend where southerly wind blows flat on lee bank. Water slow and shallow, but in length of 60 or 70 yds. ten or eleven quite decent trout moving. Cannot make out what they are taking after twenty minutes with fine-meshed net, so put up double cypher red quill. In lull in wind get fly right to good fish and get him. In next lull hook and lose another. Sorry I brought out soft rod instead of little Leonard, as I cannot command the wind. Miss several fish. Put down others because cannot manage wind. Presently hook and lose another good fish; go over length second time. Find three fish have begun again. Get one and put rest down. Catch young blackbird in landing-net. Very fierce young person. Pecks my hand savagely. Curious thrush-like markings on breast. Will disappear later. On round bend, but find no fish moving or even lying up under banks for half a mile. Suddenly stumble over one and put him down. Sit down and eat lunch, and wait, as his position is good, and he is sure to be back soon. Presently he is hovering again, rises occasionally, and moves to and fro. Offer him red quill. Put it over him perfectly three times. No offer. He continues to feed. Still bigger fish begins to rise four or five yards above. No fly on water. Offer lower fish: dull orange nymph, moistening it in mouth to make it sink. Attachment effected first chuck. Lovely yellow fish, and puts up beautiful fight. Tackle upper fish next, cast a foot short, become aware of check to line and strike—alas, too hard. Trout keeps fly. Then weeds, weeds, weeds! Off to side stream, but all are shaved bare, and, getting no encouragement, adjourn till evening. About half-past seven arrive where I began in morning, but the trout had been there for what was driven by the wind, and were not there now. Got big grayling and moderate one while waiting for trout to rise, but they were backward. About a quarter to nine saw blue-winged olive on water, and put up big orange quill; in next twenty minutes hooked six bankers, lost two, returned one and killed a leash. Great help to rapid fishing, necessary at such times, is a piece of amadou—stuff used by dentists as styptic to stop bleeding or dry teeth: quite cheap and bought in sheets—sort of fungus. Roll fly in it and it is dry in moment. Put on to this tip by a Berkshire parson. Grateful. He told me it was most effectual in saving delicate-winged mayflies dressed with summer duck, and that he had killed twenty brace on Pang with six flies in his hat, and they looked almost new. Curious how helpless a hooked trout seems at night—such a contrast to the daytime fish which goes off with "Goodbye, old man, sorry to be in such a hurry; but you must really let go my buttonhole. Have business abroad."

Saturday, 22nd July.

My last day. Sorry to see several summer snipe about meadows. Never do any good when they flit about calling their plaintive cry. This morning, thank goodness, though much in evidence, they are not calling. Still no rain; wind westerly; and glare and heat worse, if anything, than ever. Determine to go down to that lee shore again, but stop on way to see if trout which kept my nymph is in position. Sure enough there he is hovering near the surface and feeding. Offer him a Pope's green nondescript—a fly often very taking at beginning of a rise, though I could never tell why—and get him. Stop to reduce the weight of mineral-water bottle in my bag, as it is more oppressive where it is. Just beginning to tackle nice trout a little above tussock when down comes torrent of weeds. Move on up above where cutters began. No fly all morning, but just here and there one or two fish in position and apparently ready to feed. One quite close in to east bank. Drop red quill 12 or 18 in. above him. He sails out to inspect it and lets it pass, and returns to his place. Next chuck it drops absolutely right, 2 in.

above him, and between him and the bank, as if it fell from the overhanging herbage of the bank—R.I.P. *Obit* 22, vii, 1911. A few yards further on a big grayling was evidently out for mischief, and fell violently on the red quill at the first offer. His attachment was too strong, and he, too, perished. Presently I came to a broad and muddy ditch, with no bridge; but above it, in a weed pocket, within a long cast, lay a nice trout, which for several days I had in vain covered from the other side. He, too, was hovering, but not breaking the surface. The quill fell as it should, and he took it, but with three successive jumps in the air he removed himself from the jurisdiction, not a little to my chagrin, as I should have liked to get two old friends in one day.

After that I found three or four more fish—all good trout—hovering in just the same way. Every one accepted the red quill with the most confiding simplicity, and every one kicked off with more or less ceremony. Finally, there was one that did not—and so in to dinner, much occupied with speculations what the trout took the red quill for, and why they will take it when they are nymphing when they will not take an imitation of the natural fly that is the outcome of the nymphs on which the trout are feeding. None of my fish disgorged a winged fly, and I could not help wondering whether there is not, after all, something in a theory which I once sportively offered "Hyandry" that the red quill is taken for a nymph—perhaps just bursting its shuck, disclosing its wings, and about to escape. Keeper said red ant was on—in evening—so spent half an hour trying it, but in vain. Evening rise short tonight, but not too short to afford time to persuade a leash of good trout and a biggish grayling into the net. Orange quill again. The orange quill is a great institution. So I take down my rod at the end of my week, not entirely dissatisfied with my three and a half, two, three and a half, four, four and four—total, twenty-one—brace for six successive days.

Sunday, 23rd July.

Meadows dreaming with heat. Horses so beaten by it they stood head to tail in pairs under trees, and whisked each other's noses with their tails. Is it in preparation for this heat and to prevent a fly scourge that there is an enormous stock of young toads loose among the grass? Despite the heat, trout feeding steadily in the mill-head. Watch two brace closely for nearly two hours, feeding steadily, constantly breaking surface, but never, so far as I could see, taking floating fly. Occasionally flies rose from surface, but the air was so dry they seemed to be in flight as they hatched. One of the fish jumped with a whirr of tail, apparently missing in the air a small pale dun. I watched carefully for spinners, but there were none on the water, though between eight and nine I found a spider's web overhanging the surface containing fifteen tiny spinners (of four shades of medium to pale olive) and four duns of three varieties, all alive. Probably these were early-morning folk who had disported themselves during the cool of the morning. Amused to think that there are lots of riparian owners and lessees who would think it immoral to fish these subaqueous fish with anything but a rigidly dry fly. Don't think I saw a floating natural dun taken during the whole blazing week.

Farewell

———◄○►———

I RESIGNED my rod on the Abbotts Barton length of the Itchen at the end of the 1938 season. Having fished that water (which the late W. Senior described as the most difficult water within his experience—a very wide one) since May 1883, some fifty-six seasons. For many seasons before that I had not fished for trout there during September, having found September trout increasingly easy as the month advanced, most of the trout captured in September being hen fish more or less advanced in spawn and greedily feeding up in preparation for the spawning season. So my last visit was in the last week-end in August 1938.

Getting down to the river for the evening I found a tearing north-north-west gale driving down the river, much too violent to be cast against with my 9-ft. 5-oz. Leonard split cane. Several experiences in the past had taught me that, though such a gale might be sufficient to sweep every hatching fly off the water that did not necessarily involve one's leaving the water with empty creel, but that there was on such occasions the possibility of a big fish, if one could find his whereabouts, though he would be unlikely to disclose it by rising to a natural fly and to attract him a big fly was needed. I accordingly whipped on a large woodcock and orange sedge tied to float and took my way from the middle of the fishery, where the main river and the side stream most nearly approach, down the west bank of the main in the direction of McCaskie's Corner, near which I had grounds for suspecting the presence of a three-pounder—under the east bank near the corner where the swans often nested. But, though I kept a sharp look-out on every likely hatching spot under the east bank, I was offered no temptation to cast, until I was only a few yards above McCaskie's Corner where the main stream makes a sharp right-angled turn towards the little stone church of Winnal St. Magdalen. Then just as I was considering winding up and giving in I became aware of a little area of water about a yard square and about a yard from the east bank, and a trifle above the point of land facing McCaskie's Corner, where the gale catching the stream in its eastward turn produced a queer little tangle on the surface, and in this little area no fewer than three trout were feeding greedily, though no fly was to be marked on the surface. The rise forms, however, were characteristic of a taking of blue-winged olive nymph. However, in view of the gale, I did not think it necessary to change my fly, but cast it across and downstream with the wind, to alight just on the far side of the

last edge of the area described. The line lit taut and was caught by the stream and dragged the fly nicely cocked so that it was skating across the little area towards mid-stream when it was grabbed, notwithstanding the pronounced drag, by a strong trout, with a savage swirl. It was hardly necessary to strike, and in a moment I had turned the fish away so that his struggles should not scare either of the others, and presently, some little way downstream off McCaskie's Corner, I netted him out and hurried back to my stance above the corner. To my delight both of the other two trout were undisturbed and feeding as greedily as ever. I did not trouble to dry my fly, but it was of no consequence, for the next cast found me leading number two by the nose out of the little square to be netted out like number one.

Still number three was undisturbed until the woodcock orange lit at the next cast within reach of his greedy nib, when he, too, met his fate.

The first trout weighed 3 lb. 1 oz., number two was 2 lb. 9 oz. and number three was 1 lb. 13 oz. Total for the leash, 7 lb. 7 oz.

Then I turned back, bidding farewell to McCaskie's Corner, and went on, seeing no sign of any other fish to attract a cast, knowing that it was the end of my long association with that attractive water and regretting that McCaskie had not had that occasion for *his* last day.

Index